Dedication

To Marjorie Elizabeth McLaren, 1916–1999, who made me write.

Table of Contents

Acknowledgements

I have had many mentors in NLP. Phillip Brew and Nichola Farnum were the first. They gave me my first experience and taught me the basics. John McWhirter has always been an inspiration, particularly for his work on NLP models. He and Will MacDonald took me through Practitioner and Master Practitioner. I learned more conventional NLP from Frank Bentley and Peter McNab, who pushed me into understanding what a trainer is. And I have had insights through the books, videos and workshops of many other practitioners and trainers, especially the founders of NLP, Richard Bandler and John Grinder.

I would also like to thank the voluntary workers of the NLP Community, especially the Association for NLP (contact Gordon Lorraine on 0870 787 1978 or call up the website on www.anlp.org for more information on ANLP) and the Committee of the Central London NLP Practice Group (www.nlpgroup.freeserve.co.uk).

Foreword

Why are some people more effective at communicating than others? We all have pretty much the same ability to see and hear what is going on in the world around us. The main difference seems to be in what we do with this experience.

In NLP we emphasise the importance of adding or creating choice. Choice, though, is more complex than often realised. I find it useful to distinguish between three levels of choice. The first is choosing between alternatives, a simple example being the different alternatives on a menu. Choosing in this instance is from a variety of the same type of thing. The second is choosing the range of alternatives; this creates options. For example the particular restaurant and menu can be one of a number of options. The third is choosing the range of options; this creates the main choices. At this level one is selecting to go for a meal from a range of other choices such as going to the theatre, movies, staying at home.

It is important to me that people learn to learn and that they learn to be in charge of their own learning. This is only possible if all three levels of choice are available. Too often we are limited to doing more of the same. We can easily have the illusion of acquiring new choices when all we have is only an increase in alternatives. Many business models operate like this. Only with more understanding of the underlying processes can more options and choices be created. This book offers a range of skills and models that when practised will give you a full range of increased alternatives, relevant options and new and exciting choices for effective communication. How you use them will determine how effective you will be with them.

Communication excellence is a mixture of three levels of excellence. The first is to be clever in the selection of the best and most effective alternatives. The temptation to be clever is itself a potential trap. The avoidance of this trap is through the next level of excellence, the intelligent creation of choice from a wider set of options. The third and deepest level of excellence is to apply wisdom in the creation and selection of the basic choices themselves. All three of these levels are necessary.

The skills and models you will explore in this book are both clever and can, through the examples given, be more easily applied intelligently. It is in the hands of the reader to apply their own wisdom to the application. Ian has brought together many of the tried and tested NLP techniques and models. The format is innovative and a clever application of NLP in offering an opportunity to experience the exercises and descriptions from a number of perspectives. Formal training offers many things not possible in a book. Ian, however, goes a long way to overcome this with his novel format and thoughtful comments throughout. The obvious drawback of any book about communication is the lack of 'live' communication. Ian balances this by constantly introducing a variety of different responses through the dialogue between Ian's character and the participants. Connecting the different responses to a larger business context is also useful in keeping the individual responses relevant and more easily connected to all levels of communication in business. The dialogues can also guide the reader to reflect their own responses to the exercises. This will help compensate for the lack of supervision and coaching that a workshop could provide.

One of the benefits of a book over formal training is the opportunity to explore at your own pace, allowing you to take the time you need to reflect and question. All too often learning skills in a workshop with people who are all committed to the skills being successful, can give the false impression that techniques always work and that everyone will respond the same. Communication excellence requires a unique response for each person, as each person is unique. This book is definitely not an over-simplistic 'one model fits all' approach. Through the creation of diverse participants in business training Ian is able to contrast examples of the variety of needs and responses. This reduces the likelihood of the reader being left with simplifications and thus makes it more likely that you will be able to achieve success with the skills in the real world.

This book will be a very practical experience and form the basis for continued learning. In writing this book Ian shows wisdom in not 'hyping' NLP, choosing instead to guide the reader to explore and test their own experience. This realistically opens up the variety of possible responses that make it more realistic and 'human' than many books on NLP. There is an intelligent coverage of the main NLP topics each related to a main area of communication. This, together with the clever format, makes for an excellent package for the beginner and intermediate student of NLP, as well as a useful addition for anyone interested in improving their communication.

The skills you will learn here can be a major addition to your communication excellence and a major enhancement to your quality of life. Use them wisely.

John McWhirter
Certified Master Trainer of NLP

Introduction

How excellent is your communicating? Are you always understood fully at home, in the office, talking to a client? What have misunderstandings cost you? Have you lost affection, respect or a contract?

Let me tell you a story. A friend of mine, John, is happily married, with a management job in the City. Early last year, John had a bad day. It all started at breakfast time. Let's hear from his son, Sam.

> "I tried to tell Daddy but he wouldn't listen. I had been picked to play for the football team for the first time on Saturday. It was important to me – I hoped he would come to watch. But every time I tried to tell him, he turned away and did something else. All he did was tell me to stop shouting. He doesn't love me any more."

John reached the office, and was discussing the day's appointments with his secretary, Mary. Suddenly, there was another row. This is what she said:

> "I had warned John to keep the afternoon free, because his boss, Mr Harold, had scheduled an appraisal interview. It was the only time Mr Harold had free that week. That morning, John told me that he had arranged to visit an important client in Birmingham. I asked him why he hadn't asked if the afternoon was clear: he insisted that he had. He claimed I never kept him in touch. That's my job and I do it well, so I got annoyed. It's difficult to respect someone who acts like that."

Later in the morning, he had a meeting with another client, Henry Jones. They were supposed to agree the details of an important contract between their firms. But the deal wasn't done. Henry Jones put his side of the matter:

> "I have dealt with John for some time, and it is always difficult to reach agreement with him. He knows that we need his services, and the contract is always fine in general terms. But there are always details that I need to get right,

and he will never listen. He always thinks that the specific issues can be dealt with later. This time they couldn't, and I told him so. He wouldn't take me seriously, so I refused to sign the contract."

Communicating with other people includes informing them, influencing them, selling to them, leading them and helping them. It also means hearing them, learning from them, loving and respecting them. How much more will you be able to achieve when you have found excellent ways of communicating?

We are all interested in communicating with other people – our family and friends, work colleagues, bosses and officials. We need to talk to them – in person or on the phone – write to them or address them in meetings.

As you read this book and carry out the exercises, you will find new ways to get through to other people, and consolidate your existing skills. We will consider both general principles and detailed techniques such as building rapport and changing beliefs.

Communication excellence is about connecting with other people, finding out their point of view, and convincing them to do something you want them to do. These activities we will call *matching*, *pacing* and *leading*. If you can set your outcomes, put yourself in the right state, believe in what you are doing and have the skills at your fingertips, you will improve your dealings with anyone you come across.

We will be looking at examples at home, at work and at leisure. You may want a clearer insight into your own actions, beliefs and values, or to know more about others. You may want to sell to others or buy from them, teach or understand, attract them or push them away.

We will be approaching new material in small chunks, as well as considering the wider applications. That means that you will be able to build up your understanding in steps that suit you. Don't forget that we all communicate when we are with anyone else, so we have all had years of practice. What this book does is to make you aware of what you are doing, and consider how you might do it more effectively.

Techniques of this type are often called manipulative, implying that they are unethical. Manipulation – teaching, selling or inspiring – is one purpose of communication. What you do with it must fit in with your own ethics and conscience – nothing in this book will encourage you to change them for the worse.

You will, no doubt, have some questions. Let's start with something fairly obvious. Why should you learn more about communicating? There is a common belief that we can always learn more about any subject. By learning more, we can do it better. And we can feel better about knowing more and using new skills. Just take a moment to consider those occasions in the past when you could have communicated better. You might have said something that upset your partner or a friend. Remember the times when you missed a sale or some other advantage by misunderstanding the other person. Think of times when you failed to get your point across clearly. Now look forward to being able to handle those situations with skill and enjoyment.

Let's go back and find out how John coped with the results of his bad day. The first thing he had to sort out was the contract with Henry Jones. John finally realised that when you are leading someone to do something that is important to you, like signing a valuable contract, you have to tell your client what he wants to hear. If it is important for that person, it must also be important for you. John didn't have to concede anything important from a financial or business standpoint. He did have to acknowledge that he was wrong and his client was right.

So how did he work to regain the respect of his secretary, Mary? What she wanted was to pass on the information that she had. John needed to pace her. Once they had calmed down, they quickly agreed a new system for keeping each other aware of important information, with written backup in case either of them should forget what they had been told. As John began to acknowledge Mary's skills, her respect for him was rebuilt.

John went to the football match on Saturday, but he was aware that his son wasn't happy. Sam kept saying that his father didn't love him because he wouldn't listen. John was confused. He thought that he was a good listener. He could keep up with all the family gossip and read the newspaper at the same time. They could ask him questions about it. It was his wife who pointed out that people like to be matched. He needed to look at the person he was in conversation with, show he was following by using their tones and words, and look interested.

That was when John came to me to tell me this story, and to learn about rapport.

The book will give you a full list of instructions so that you can understand, learn and practise ways of improving your communicating. We shall learn about matching, and the techniques of rapport. You will find out about pacing to gather information about the other person. There will be examples of how to lead to where you both want to go. There will be plenty of exercises, and sources for much of the material, so that you can extend your learning.

The structure of the book is a ten-lesson course in communications held for the staff of a (fictitious) company, Whizzitts Ltd. We will work through examples of communicating from their working and private lives. To get the most out of the book, you should work though the techniques and exercises as they come up. Often, a skill that you learn in one chapter will be a necessary of another technique that is developed later. For example, the skills of *outcome-setting*, *self-pacing* and *rapport* are needed for any kind of communicating.

The book is organised to give you the chance to decide where you can use the techniques in your everyday life. We will point out some of the applications, and ask you to think about how else you will apply the skills that you have learned. There are also suggestions about further skills, and information and ways of acquiring it.

So what are you going to learn? The choice is yours. The book provides a context from which you can draw what you need. Let's hear what a few of the course participants had to say about the experience. We'll start with the views of Amanada Prescott.

"As soon as we started the course, we could see what we were doing wrong. A lot of what we did was inappropriate to the people we were with, and the situation. We weren't looking at the person to match them or find out about what was going on for them. We weren't watching where they were going, so we missed the chance to grab their attention. As we learned more, I became much more aware of what was going on, and could change what I was doing to match, pace and lead my partners. You can't really lead people until you can see what they are doing and be clear about what you want them to do. That's my contribution."

Now we'll let PS Scarlet tell his story.

"I must say that at the beginning of the process I didn't really believe that talking about communicating would get us very far. Then I heard how the language that we use affects others – what they hear and how much they miss. We all represent the world differently and have different preconceptions and presuppositions about it. I learned a lot about how to use words that people will understand, and how to get my language to sound right. If we are going to teach, the information we give has to fit with the knowledge and understanding that the person already has."

Vanessa Greenage will give us her feelings on the course.

"It's very important to me how I feel, and I now know that the same is true for everyone else. The emotional content of what they communicate may not fit in with our normal pattern. We need to make adjustments. If we want to encourage and inspire others, we have to find out about their values and triggers before we can suggest things that will fit in with them."

We can know what we want: we can only guess what others want. If we are going to direct, teach, sell to, inspire and encourage others we have to refine our model of their world and present our material in the light of it. I asked our participants what is important to them about communicating well. This is a list of their answers. They are all right, and all necessary.

"Being aware of their state and emotions"
"Getting your mood right, then getting their mood right"

"Respecting their values in what you say"
"Using their language"
"Finding out their presuppositions and beliefs"
"Fitting your new information into what they already know"
"Matching their physiology"
"Calibrating what their posture, expression and movements mean"
"Directing them with your whole body"

The tools in the book are drawn from the results of work in psychology and linguistics. They come from the science of subjective experience called Neuro-Linguistic Programming or NLP. This originated in the 1970s as a way of studying therapists, and is now being widely applied in business, particularly to improve interpersonal communication.

I think that it's about time to meet the course participants:

The course *presenter* is **Ian McLaren**. That's him in the bright red shirt, trying to get the whiteboard pens to work. He is a registered INLPTA Trainer of Neuro-Linguistic Programming. His background is in financial and general management. After qualifying with a BSc in Economics and Accounting and an MSc in Operational Research from the University of Hull, he became an Investment Manager. As Investment Controller and Planner with the Canada Life Assurance Company, he worked in London, New York and Toronto, gaining a wide range of senior management experience. In the 1990s, he has been a finance director, consultant, author, business coach and trainer.

The representatives of Whizzitts Ltd are:

The Chairman, *Sir John* Sapphire-Smith is tall and distinguished. He is in his early sixties, and smartly dressed as if for a business meeting. He is slightly distant in manner, but contributes freely to the discussions.

Prudence Plum is the Managing Director. She is busy and slightly harassed-looking. Prudence is quite tall, but tries to look inconspicuous. She favours formal suits in autumnal colours.

PS
John   Ruth   Harry   Stephen   Paul
Amanada   Ian   Prudence   Sir John   Apricot   Vanessa

Group Photograph: The Whizzitt's Team

The Marketing Director is *Apricot* Peach. In contrast to her managing director, she is young, active and brightly and fashionably dressed. Tall, slim, and tanned, she is always confidently at the centre of things.

Whizzitts have an American Sales Director, *PS* (Pius Sears) Scarlet. Tall and sharply dressed, he radiates friendliness and *bonhomie*. His favourite pastime is talking.

Stephen Navy runs the production operations. He was a rugby player for his college and county, and looms large and square in his customary sports shirt and blue blazer. Competence, rather than brilliance, is his forte.

The Human Resources chief is *Vanessa* Greenage. She is middle-aged, middle size and tends to dress in tweeds and knitwear. Her role seems to be agony aunt.

Amanada Prescott, who comes from the West Indies, is in her early twenties. She runs the sales office. She also helps out with her boyfriend's independent record company and sings with a band, which is trying to break into the big time.

Legal executive *Harry* Smith is normally casually dressed. He often complains about not being allowed to smoke in the sessions.

John Robinson is a computer programmer. He is also casually dressed and tends to remain in the background.

Paul Pointer is a sales engineer. He is in his early thirties and likes smart clothes.

Secretary *Ruth* Rutherford looks after a young daughter. She needs some drawing out before she will contribute.

You can sit where you like in the group, and join in with all the exercises. The more that you practise, the more you will learn.

So what next? Once you are more aware of your outcomes, you will find yourself getting on better with other people, making stronger relationships, selling yourself and your products and services. You can then think back to the difference that it has made to develop and practise all those new and extended skills. And you'll be able to think how else you can use the techniques you have learned...

Day One: Understanding Yourself

Welcome to the first day of this course, everyone. Special thanks to the management of Whizzitts Ltd, who have allowed us to share in this course, and for agreeing that we can use some examples from their firm as illustrations. This course will include a series of suggestions and exercises using a number of tools to help you improve how you talk, listen or write to other people. At the end of each day, I want to leave you with some ideas and some things to practise as you go about your normal life at work, at home or at leisure.

This is what we are going to cover in this lesson:

• *Communicating*
Communicating is what we say to people, how we say it and how we listen, why it is we are talking to them. From a company's point of view, the messages that we are putting out to staff, customers, financiers and the world, and the feedback we read or hear, is all part of corporate communication.

• *Pacing Yourself*
As we shall learn, the state you are in has a very powerful effect on the way that you think and believe. We shall learn a way of finding calm and concentration that can be useful when starting conversations.

• *Doing, Thinking and Feeling*
Just consider what happens when you are talking to someone. You are doing things – speaking, gesturing, listening, sitting or standing. You are thinking of things – what the other person is saying, what you are going to say, and possibly how to get away for your next appointment. You are also feeling things – nervous about making the sale, angry because you are not being understood, happy about the news the other person is bringing you or wondering what will happen next. Technically, we can talk about *External Behaviour* – what we are doing, how someone is standing, their expression, voice tones and actions. We will look at *Internal Process* – how we think, believe, know and process information, and how we use language. You should also consider *Internal State* – how you feel, what you value, people's emotions, criteria and attitudes. We also need to be aware of the *Environment* – the place, time and conditions in which or about which a conversation is taking place:

who else is there and what else is going on. Each of these can affect the course and the outcome of a conversation.

• *Perceiving*

We don't know 'the truth'; we only know what we can perceive. We automatically fill in the gaps by guessing, extrapolating and reading between the lines. You can do this consciously to give yourself new insights by stepping into other people's shoes. We will demonstrate and learn a formal way of doing this called the *Meta-Mirror*.

• *Time and Space*

Humans usually represent time in the form of pictures that seem to be located in space. We will find out how you see the past and the future in your *Time Lines*.

• *Setting Objectives*

We all have a number of things that we want or intend to do. Some of them get done, many do not. The process of setting a *Well-Formed Outcome* will allow you to decide what your *Positive* and *Measurable* outcome is. Achieving it will depend on whether you have the *Resources* (time, money, skills, etc.) and *Control* (can you do it all yourself?), and whether you judge the *Consequences* to be acceptable. Then you can *Plan* and *Timetable* achieving it.

Communicating

We all communicate, and do it much of the time. You are in touch with yourself and with other people. It happens at work, at home, and in your social life. And sometimes we are unhappy with the results, whether we are trying to lead, teach or inspire; to sell some goods or ideas or to motivate. Good communicating has a strategy behind it, whether we are writing an article for the staff magazine, talking to our partner or pushing for an answer from a customer.

Before we go into detail about communicating, let's hear about some typical situations, and what might be improved. Sir John, would you like to give us an overview of Whizzitts Ltd?

"Thank you. My name is Sir John Sapphire-Smith. I am a main board director of Amalgamated Conglomerate Holdings plc. We set up Whizzitts Ltd about ten years ago, when the market for smaller electric whizzers first took off. For most of that time we have been number two in the market, which has grown tenfold since we started. Now, cheap Far Eastern producers are about to enter the market. This will drive down our margins unless we can restructure the way we operate. Basically we have two choices. We could transfer all our whizzer production to cheaper sites, and just deal with sales and service in the UK. Or we could cut our production costs here, switch as far as possible to the highest-value lines, and rely on having better design and features. As Chairman of the company, I am finally responsible for that choice, and for making sure that the management and other structures are in place to implement it."

So here we have communicating on the macro-scale. Sir John has to find out what is best for the whole company to do, and then get everyone in the company to work to implement that plan. And the communicating won't just be inside Whizzitts Ltd – he may have to deal with overseas contractors, outside suppliers, customers and the board of the parent company.

Perhaps Apricot could give us some idea of what this means from inside the company?

"OK, I'm Apricot Peach, the Marketing Director of Whizzitts Ltd, one of the most successful companies that this country has ever produced. It's my job to make sure that when people want a whizzer they think of buying the best-quality Whizzitts whizzer. All right, advert over. We have to think our way through the next few years, really believing in ourselves and in what we sell. We have to learn new skills, invent new products and teach the customers to need them. We're all going to have to work long and hard to achieve the right results."

Apricot is concerned with what people think, believe and know. Again, that involves outsiders – not only suppliers and customers, but also families, especially if the employees are going to be working longer hours.

5

Vanessa Greenage is the Human Resources Director of Whizzitts. Vanessa, could you tell us about the staff?

> "Hello, I'm Vanessa. We've always been a close-knit team, and everyone is involved. Even though we have grown so fast – there are still less than a hundred of us in total – most of the actual manufacturing is done outside. My job is to influence the state of morale to make sure that we can all feel comfortable with whatever plan is decided on, and that no-one is left out in the cold. If we are properly motivated, I'm sure that we can be inspired to meet the demands of the new plan."

Vanessa's priorities are to make sure that people have the right feelings in the organisation. Change is difficult on an emotional level, and efficiency can be badly affected if the staff feel unhappy about what is going on.

We'll find out what issues other people have during the course of the day – perhaps you would like to write some of your concerns down now. They may not be as large as those at Whizzitts Ltd, but we are all facing changes of one sort or another, which can cause stress with what we do, how we think or the way we feel. As we have seen, the main change may be at work, but it can affect all our relationships: with our bosses and staff, customers and suppliers, family and friends.

Yes, John?

> "This may sound a small point, but I want to get my boss to give me a decent raise this year. Is this a communications issue?"

John has found a very useful topic to summarise the whole subject of communicating. Just think what you do in order to get a pay rise. Your prime aim is to get your boss to *do* something – to make sure you get more money coming in each month. You may also want to get them to *believe* something – that you are worth a higher salary, or that you will leave if you don't get one. Or you may want the boss to *feel* that you are worth more, or that the business could not get on without you. And the way that you persuade the company of your value is also through communication. You might *act* –

apply for another job, walk out or arrange a sit-in at reception. You might *teach* the management what you can contribute to the success of the firm. You might *inspire* them by your contribution to the business. But if you don't communicate, you won't achieve the rise.

Exercise 1.1: Your Communication Issues

Now, can you get a piece of paper and spend a few minutes writing down at least three of your own Communication Issues? We will keep coming back to these throughout the course.

In every communication, there is period of *matching*, when we find the best way of getting through to the other person. Then a period of *pacing*, when we find out what they are doing, how they understand the issue and what they feel about it. Finally, there is a period of *leading*, when we influence that person to change what they are doing, thinking or feeling. This process of matching, pacing and leading underlies NLP, which has been called the science of excellence in communication. NLP was first codified in America in the 1970s, although it includes many earlier ideas. We will be using NLP and similar techniques and exercises all through this course. There is a source list at the end of the book.

Pacing Yourself

Let's start with our internal communicating. We are not going to get through to others very easily if we can't listen to ourselves and have internal harmony. Perhaps you find that you are very agitated just before you meet people. Maybe you cannot give your attention to them because you are listening to the voices inside your head rather than to what they are saying. Or you are making lots of pictures of what might happen, so that the actual event gets confused.

Exercise 1.2: Pacing Yourself

The *self-pacing* exercise is very simple, and takes only a few seconds. You can use it to calm your thoughts and focus on your outcome for the meeting that is coming up. Just work through it a few times until you are comfortable to use it anywhere.

Start by getting up and moving around; shake out any stiffness. Now sit down again, with your back straight and head upright; both feet flat on the floor. Become aware of your breathing, and of the dialogue going on inside your head. Breath through your nose, if that is comfortable, and be aware of the temperature of the air – colder as you breathe in, warmer as you breathe out. Be aware of the room around you, but keep your focus on your breathing. Be aware that as your breathing slows, the activity in your head becomes less frenetic and more relaxed. Then you can take that sense of internal calm into your external communicating.

In future, use self-pacing whenever you need to be able to listen well. This calm state might be particularly useful before important business meetings, making sales or presentations. You might also want to use it if that next encounter with your partner or friend is likely to end in a row. You can think of some specific examples in your life. Just imagine yourself having done the self-pacing technique, and then having communicated so much more effectively with that important person. Yes, that was much better, wasn't it?

Doing, Thinking and Feeling

Let's test out your powers of memory and imagination. Remember a time when you were having a conversation with someone. It doesn't matter where it was, when it happened or what you were talking about. Now, imagine you are having that conversation now.

OK, what did you notice? First of all, we will consider what you were *doing*. You were talking, listening, looking. Some of you will have been aware of the way you were standing or sitting, the wind or sun on your skin, the papers in your hand. Perhaps you were smoking or drinking; smiling or frowning; walking or driving.

Next, let's see what you were *thinking*. Information was coming in and going out. You may have been analysing or pondering over it, or you might have been thinking about something completely different. Somewhere in your head, the ideas were being put into language, amounts calculated, knowledge accumulated. You might have talked about what you believed, or disagreed with the beliefs that you heard from the other person.

Then there was the way that you were *feeling*. Did you like or hate the other person? Were you elated or bored, excited or depressed? Could you tell what he or she was feeling? All sorts of things in the situation might have affected what you felt – were your values or criteria being violated? Did you share the same attitudes? Do you have the same type of personality?

Now consider the *circumstances* of the conversation. Think of where and when it happened, what went before it and what else was going on. Would the conversation have been the same if the *situation* had been different? Is talking to your boss the same in her office as it is on the beach?

It has been clear to cognitive psychologists for some time that our mind and body are part of the same system. Anything that we do changes the way we think and feel, and the other way round. If we stand in front of a fire, we may feel uncomfortably warm and think we should move away. If we *think* we are standing in front of a blazing fire (even if it is not actually true, say in a dream), we may feel uncomfortable, our skin temperature can rise, and we may try to move away. If we *feel* uncomfortably warm, we may believe that we should move away from the fire, and actually do so, even if our skin temperature is not actually raised.

In NLP, we summarise this relationship in the Mercedes Model, from work done by Leslie Cameron-Bandler. The model shown in Handout 1.1 assumes that any individual reacts to an event in a particular environment or situation by changing External Behaviour (EB), Internal Process (IP) or Internal State (IS).

We have already found out that these three factors are strongly linked. A change in any one is likely to lead to changes in the rest. If I change from nodding to shaking my head, you are likely to say something different and feel differently. The environment and situation are also likely to make a difference. Let's say I ask you to walk ten feet with your eyes closed in return for a fee of £100. Situation One is in the middle of an empty football field.

Situation Two is on the yardarm of HMS *Victory*. Are the way you act, what you think, and your state of mind likely to be the same in both cases?

Let's apply this to some business communications issues. Stephen, you can give us an example?

> "Yes. Hi, I'm Stephen Navy. I'm in charge of production at Whizzitts Ltd. That means keeping control of all the sub-contractors and running the final assembly line. We have problems with one of the contractors, who keeps running late with deliveries and holding up production."

OK, you want them to do something differently. You have a number of choices. Whizzitts Ltd could change the *situation*, by getting a new subcontractor. You might change their *behaviour* directly, by helping them to improve their production or delivery systems. An alternative would be to train them to deliver on time, getting them to *believe* that it is important to have the parts there at the right time. Or you could change their *values*, perhaps by rewarding them with a bonus for being on time.

Does someone have an issue about beliefs? Yes, Vanessa?

> "Right. The personnel department is responsible for the Whizzitts company newsletter. We send it out, and then try to find out what the employees think about it. But the feedback I get suggests that most of them don't believe what they are being told by management, and very few of them read it."

And if they did read it, they might learn something useful to them? Again, you could change the *situation* – you could have live meetings or a corporate video, so they would *do* something different. The company could *teach* them to use the information they were being given, so they would read the newsletter to *learn* about developments. Or you could improve their *feelings* about the newsletter by adding content that interests them, and by presenting the management contributions in a way that seems true and makes sense to them.

Handout 1.1: MERCEDES MODEL

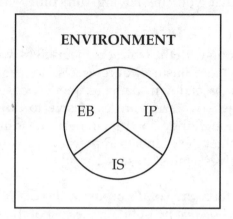

EXAMPLES:

EB - External Behaviour	IP - Internal Process	IS - Internal State
Doing –	**Thinking –**	**Feeling –**
Sensing:	**Language:**	**Values:**
Vision	Words	Towards
Hearing	Grammars	Away from
Touching	Vocabularies	Good
Smelling	Metaphors	Bad
Tasting	Similes	**Criteria:**
Expressing:	**Abstraction:**	Sameness/Difference
Face	Time	Size
Posture	Maps	Contexts
Skin Colour	Models	Exclusivity
Muscle Tension	Diagrams	**Attitudes:**
Gestures	Groups	Curiosity
Breathing:	**Mathematics:**	Flexibility
Position	Calculation	Wonder
Rate	Logic	Exploration
Pauses	Geometry	Presuppositions
Speaking:	Sets	**Emotions:**
Tone	Statistics	Love
Pace	**Beliefs:**	Hate
Pitch	Personal	Pain
Moving:	Identity	Joy
Manipulation	Spiritual	Anxiety
Walking	**Learning:**	Depression
Voluntary Actions	Assembling	Elation
Complex Actions	Knowledge	Excitement

11

Finally, we should look at a question concerned with values. PS, I believe that you are having difficulties with some of your customers.

> "Yes. Along with the whizzers themselves, we also sell maintenance and insurance contracts, to protect the clients against breakdown, damage, theft and so on. These are valuable – whizzers are expensive to buy and to repair, even though they don't often need mending. But it is very hard to get the clients to appreciate the value of protecting themselves against this risk."

OK, again there are some corporate choices. Whizzitts Ltd could change the *situation* by building the cost of the warranties into the price that you charge for the machine "Free maintenance, damage repairs and insurance for three years." You could *do* something to show how vulnerable the whizzers are to theft or damage. Maybe you could do more to *persuade* the clients of the costs that they might incur – sample bills, or whatever. Or you might *influence* them by telling them how other customers felt when they couldn't afford to get their whizzers replaced or mended.

Exercise 1.3: Analysing Your Issue

Get together with some other people if you can. Use the sheets you filled out in Exercise 1.1. Take one of your Communications Issues. The group should spend a few minutes discussing the issue and consider whether it is to do with external behaviour, internal processing or internal state (or maybe more than one of those). Then, find a way that you might address it by each of the following:

1. Changing the environment or situation
2. Changing what you do, or doing something in order to achieve a change
3. Helping yourself or someone else to change what they think, know or believe
4. Helping yourself or others to change what they value or feel about the issue.

When that is done, move on to the next person. It will help if you keep notes for your own issue.

Have you started to get some ideas about how to address your issues? You can continue to work on them until we meet again.

Perceiving

The Metaphor is a tool that enables us to talk about something that is difficult to represent directly. We say *this* is like *that*. It won't be exactly true, but there may be enough truth in it to be useful. When we actually want to sense something, we can only do it from within. We do, however have a formal set of metaphors that allow us to pretend that we can do it differently. You cannot see most of your own face directly. What you can do is use a mirror to see an *image* of your face. More mirrors, or a video camera and screen, allow you to see the back of your head, as if you were looking through the eyes of someone standing behind you. Or you can move the camera round to the front, so that you have a picture of yourself from a distance. We have all seen these images, so you can imagine how you look as you sit in your chair now. Can you all do this? Good.

See how you look from the viewpoint of someone you are having a conversation with. Now move up into the air, and be aware of how you look from up there on the light fitting. In fact you can see everyone in the room from up here: don't they all look small? Just spend a few minutes looking at yourself and other people from all round the room. You might like to take your attention outside the building, and see yourself through the window.

Now, just imagine you are talking to someone, and disagreeing. It's someone you want or need to get on with better. You know who that would be. Now let's find out how to understand the other person better. The metaphor we use is *stepping into someone else's shoes*. Let's try that.

Can you all please think of someone with whom you want to get on better? That person might be a family member, someone at work or a customer. Remember a time when you had a conversation with them that didn't go too well. Now, imagine what it would be like if you could have that conversation with a better outcome.

Handout 1.2: The Meta-Mirror Exercise

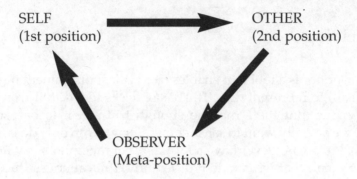

SELF
(1st position)

OTHER
(2nd position)

OBSERVER
(Meta-position)

1.   Work with another person. Play the roles of Subject and Guide, taking a turn in each role. The Subject will have a short (a few seconds) imaginary conversation with someone (called the Other) whom the Subject wants to get on better with. The Subject does not need to talk about who the Other is, or what the conversation is about. It will be easier if the Other is given a name (not necessarily the actual name). The Guide will read the instructions and help the Subject to carry them out.

2.   The Guide should help the Subject to establish the three positions shown on the diagram above – mark each of the positions (Self, Other and Observer) on the floor with a piece of paper. Make sure that each position is clearly visible from the others.

3.   The Guide should ask the Subject to stand on the Self-position, facing the Other. Then ask the Subject to remember having a conversation with the Other where the Subject would have liked a better outcome.

4.   Now ask the Subject to imagine that the Other is present. The Subject can see and hear the Other through the Subject's own eyes and ears. Ask the Subject to have that

conversation again now without speaking. Allow the Subject to finish the conversation.

5.   The Guide should get the Subject to step off the first position. Ask the Subject to take the part of the Other in the same conversation. Take the Subject to second position, and get the person to stand on it facing Self. Get the Subject to imagine seeing and hearing himself or herself standing in the first position.

6.   Ask the Subject to imagine having the same conversation, pretending to be the Other. Wait until the conversation has finished.

7.   The Guide should get the Subject to move onto the Meta-position. Ask the Subject to be a dispassionate witness of the conversation between Self and Other. Then let the Subject imagine Self and Other having the conversation, so that the Subject can find out how the exchange seems to a neutral Observer. Let the conversation come to a natural end.

8.   Ask the Subject to consider what has been learned from seeing the conversation from different angles, particularly that of a neutral observer.

9.   The Guide should bring the Subject back to the First position. Ask the Subject to have a new conversation, with a better outcome, making use of all the information that they have picked up from all the perceptual positions.

10.   Change roles, and take the new Subject through the same exercise.

Now, how could we step into someone else's shoes? How about doing it literally? Set out a pair of shoes on the floor opposite us, then go and step into them. Perhaps that's being a bit too literal – we'll put down a piece of paper where the person would stand, then we can go and step on that. When we do that, we can pretend to be that person. To show that both of us are in the conversation, we can put another piece of paper on the floor. When we stand on that spot, we are ourselves. Who else might we be? It might be nice to be able to stand back and look at what is going on. Somewhere you can observe the conversation and remain neutral. Let's mark that as well. We now have a triangle of marks, similar to the diagram at the top of Handout 1.2.

Could we have a volunteer Subject to try out this way of having a conversation? Thank you, PS. Just come out to the front. You don't need to tell us anything or speak out loud while you are doing this exercise. Please just let us know when you have finished each conversation. OK, you know whom you want to speak to, and what the topic is? Good. Just for convenience, can you give the Other a name – it needn't be the real one. OK, we'll call him Eric.

We'll follow the instructions on the handout, and I'll act as Guide. Come to the first position and look towards Eric. Now, remember the conversation, and take yourself back into it. Imagine that Eric is in front of you, and that you can see and hear him. In your own mind, go through the conversation again, and hear what Eric has to say. If you don't remember, just guess.

Good. Step off there. Now, when you get to the second position, you are going to pretend to be Eric, and take his part in the conversation. That's it, step onto the second position and face the first position. Imagine that PS is standing on the first position, and that you are inside Eric looking at PS. Now go through the conversation again, from Eric's point of view.

OK. Come over here. When you step onto the Observer-position you are going to be an independent witness of the conversation between PS and Eric. You are not involved – you might be watching a film or television programme. Just imagine PS and Eric having that conversation and be aware of everything that is going on.

Now you will have learned some lessons from seeing things from a different perspective. You might want to act differently, change the way you were thinking or alter your state and feelings. So let's try having the conversation again, bearing in mind all that you now know. Come to the first position and face Eric, and talk to him again.

Good. So how was that, compared with the original conversation?

> "I think we managed to resolve a few things. When I stepped into his shoes I realised that he was coming from a position that I was not. He had different priorities and outcomes from mine. We needed to bring that out in the open and come to a compromise. It will certainly be easier to talk to him next time."

Exercise 1.4: Seeing the Other Side
OK, it's time for everyone to have a go at the Meta-mirror exercise. Please find a partner and plenty of space to work in. Use the handout. Mark out the perceptual positions on the floor, and see the conversation from each viewpoint: as Self, as the Other and as a neutral observer, who can see both sides and offer impartial advice. The exercise should take you about 15 minutes each, so come back together in half an hour and we'll discuss the results.

Did everyone find out what it is like to take a different view of the situation, hear the words from a new direction and feel what it's like in someone else's place? If you need more advice about how to resolve the situation, try putting in an expert, who you know would have the answers. When you step into their shoes, that resource will be available for you. And if there are other people that you feel badly about, or who give you problems in communicating, then use the Meta-mirror to find out a bit more about them.

Time and Space

We often use spatial metaphors to describe how we relate to time. We talk of putting the past behind us, looking back at the past and forward to the future. Many people will see pictures relating to specific times – either in the past or the future – in specific places.

Let's find out how far this is true for each of you. First, please visualise something that you do every day, have done for some years, and will continue to do in the future. Choose something that is OK to see yourself doing – but you won't have to tell anybody what it is: just give the scene a code name that anyone can use when questioning you (for example, *Fred*).

Exercise 1.5: Time Lines

Now, to establish your *time line*, get together in pairs, and when you are clear on the exercise, find somewhere you can stand together with a bit of space around you. Choose one of you to be the Explorer; the other will be an Assistant.

The Assistant first asks the Explorer to "Please see yourself doing *Fred* today, and tell me where you represent that". The Assistant should notice if the Explorer points, or ask for details if the location is vague. It may be inside the body or head, or anywhere outside. If outside, find the position in terms of direction and distance from the body, and height above the ground. It may be helpful to move to the indicated spot, and use a hand to mark the position.

Next, find out where the Explorer represents the past. Ask him to "Please see yourself doing *Fred* a week ago, and tell me where you represent that". Mark that position. Then ask, "Please see yourself doing *Fred* a year ago, and tell me where you represent that"; and "Please see yourself doing *Fred* five years ago, and tell me where you represent that". Mark those positions. Ask the Explorer, "Can you see a line of representations of doing *Fred* linking now and five years ago?" Note the answer.

Finally, find out where the Explorer represents the future. Ask, "Please see yourself doing *Fred* next week, and tell me where you represent that". Mark that position. Then ask, "Please see yourself doing *Fred* a year from now, and tell me where you represent that"; and "Please see yourself doing *Fred* five years from now, and tell me where you represent that". Mark those positions. Ask the Explorer, "Can you see a line of representations of doing *Fred* linking now and five years ahead?" Note the answer. The Explorer should remember where their own representations are, and make notes if appropriate.

Then change roles, so that the Assistant becomes the Explorer, and repeat the exercise. This should take about 15 or 20 minutes in total. Then come back together.

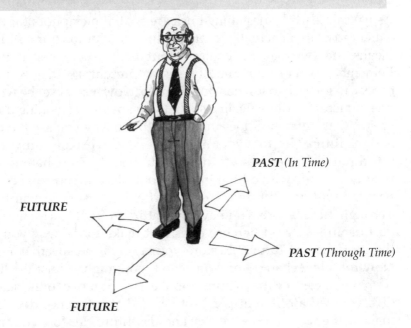

PAST (In Time)

FUTURE

PAST (Through Time)

FUTURE

Sir John finds his Timelines

OK, so what did you find? Everyone had a time line? Good. I know one or two of you struggled to find the pictures – in some cases because they weren't in sight until you turned your head. There were quite a number of different patterns – some of you keep all these representations very close to you, others have the past and the future a long way away. The pictures were at different heights – some of you could not see more than one rep-resentation at a time because they were all in a line.

There are two basic types of time lines. The one called *In Time* normally has the past behind you and the future in front. You have to make an effort to turn to see the past, and often the future pictures all appear in the same line of sight, so that few of them are visible. The present is either inside your head or very close in front. The other type is called *Through Time*. Most people with this pattern will be able to see a long line of representations, with the past on the left, the present in front and the future on the right. Some left-handed people will reverse the order. There are lots of personal variations.

As we said earlier, these time lines are spatial metaphors for time – memories aren't actually located behind you or to your left. That means that we have a choice about how we represent time. Remember where your time line is at present, so that you can choose to go back to it when you want to. Now, visualise the whole line of pictures. Move the line so that you are above, looking down on it. What difference does that make to the way you see the past and the future? Restore your normal perspective. Now, turn yourself through 90 degrees, so that if you were In Time before, you now have your whole time line in front of you. You can see the past, present and future across your field of vision. If you were Through Time before, you have the future in front of you and the past behind. What difference does that make to the way you see the past and the future? Restore your normal perspective again. Now try a few changes of your own – you might adjust the lines so that you can see the pictures more easily, or move to the side to give yourself a different perspective... What difference does that make to the way you see the past and the future? Restore your normal perspective again.

This is one example of how we can use language to move ourselves metaphorically, and change our feelings. It's something we do naturally, of course – we talk about *standing back* to look at a problem, or *focusing in* on it. How else do you think you could improve your life by taking a new perspective?

Setting Objectives

Let's put all these pieces together by talking about *outcomes*. NLP has the concept of well-formed outcomes. There is no point in having goals unless we can achieve them, and know when we have achieved them. There is even less point in having a goal that will make your life, or someone else's life, worse if you achieve it.

The Outcome Frame is a way of considering whether an outcome is well formed. The important things about an outcome are:

Positive – The outcome must be stated in the positive and include something to achieve.

Measurable – You and other people must have some way of seeing that you have achieved it.

Self – The outcome must be something you can start, have control over and can achieve.

Resources – You must have access to the necessary resources, especially time, money and skills, and be prepared to use them to achieve this outcome.

Consequences – You need to consider what effects achieving the outcome will have on you and on other people round you.

Time – When will you start and when will you achieve the outcome?

Harry, you have an example?

"Yes, I want to stop smoking. How do I put that in the positive?"

OK, let's assume for a moment that 'giving up smoking' passes all the other criteria for Harry. How will he *know* that he has stopped smoking? Perhaps a certain amount of time will have passed since he last bought a packet of cigarettes, or smoked one. Perhaps when he believes that he is an ex-smoker. Perhaps when he no longer craves the taste. So what might someone else witness? That Harry hasn't smoked for a particular period of time; that he says congruently that he is an ex-smoker or that he does not need a cigarette? Then the outcome might be stated as, "Harry will reach a time when the number of cigarettes he has smoked in the previous week is zero and he believes that he is an ex-smoker". You should probably decide how far ahead that time is.

The methodology of the well-formed outcome comes down mainly to resources and skills. You know *how* you will reach your goal if you have the necessary resources – including money, time, opportunity and motivation, and necessary skills to achieve the steps. You also need to set a timetable for achieving the goal. In this business, setting an outcome to be achieved "sometime" is the same as setting it to be achieved never.

The resources must be under your control. An outcome is not well formed if it relies on someone else (or chance). You may know how to buy a lottery ticket, and have the motivation, opportunity, time and money to do it, but you are only going to win a fortune if your numbers are drawn. Since you are not doing the drawing, it is not under your control, so setting out to win the lottery is not a well-formed outcome (unless you know something that I don't!).

For Harry, becoming an ex-smoker cannot be a well-formed outcome until he knows what steps to take, has learned to carry them out, and has assembled the necessary resources (especially motivation).

Outcomes must have a purpose. The conditions for being well formed include questions about *why* you want the outcome. Start by considering the effect of achieving your outcome on yourself and others. What will you and others gain and lose if you achieve the outcome? What will you and others gain and lose if you fail to achieve it? Does it take you towards or away from other goals? Does this form part of a larger goal? Or are there other outcomes that you need to have before you can have this one? Is there anything else that you would rather do with the resources you need for this outcome?

Let's turn back to Harry for a moment. Some of the effects on Harry of being an ex-smoker are positive – say in terms of health and money. Others might be less good – might you become more tense or abrupt? Or eat too much? And what about others round you – some of them might welcome a smoke-free atmosphere, but what about your wife? She smokes? And doesn't want to give up? I see lots of nodding. We could go on... I think you are getting the idea.

Exercise 1.6: Your Outcomes

It is time for another exercise. Please take a piece of paper and write down at least three outcomes. You should have at least one in a work context, one to do with your home life or family, and one for your leisure or social life. Go through each of the outcomes in turn, and decide whether it is correctly stated, feasible and worth having. You'll probably have to keep modifying the statement, and you may have to add details. If you make major modifications at any stage, remember to run through the other criteria again with the new goal. Take fifteen minutes for this.

Now, get together in pairs, and discuss each of the outcomes in turn. Consider all the well-formed outcome criteria, and help your partner to check that they are happy with their goals, have the resources to achieve them, and check the effects on everybody concerned. Take another half-hour for this.

Is there any feedback? I heard some of you talking about resources that are not under your control. Any time you have to rely on someone else, the outcome is not well formed. If you have to pass an interview to get a job, or put in a sealed bid to win a contract, the outcome is not under your control. The best you can do is to set up a series of possibilities, depending on the chance of success in each case. You may be able to work out how many interviews you might need in order to be certain of getting a job, or you may have some fall-back plan that doesn't involve other people.

If the part that you don't have control over is in the middle of the steps that leads up to an outcome, then you need to split the outcome into several steps. Then provide alternatives for the step that is not fully under your control. Would someone like to give us an example? Thank you, Amanada.

> "Hello, I'm Amanada. My outcome is to make a hit record. Yeah, that is a big chunk to take in one outcome. I am trained as a singer, and I do some gigs with my boyfriend and his band – pubs and so on. He writes the music and I do the words. And I see my way about the business. We have a few numbers ready, which seem to go down quite well. What I've got to do is show record producers that we

are the business. If I can't do that, we must just go on building up a following – I suppose we could get a few cassettes
recorded and try to sell them at our gigs. But it's up to our
fans whether we can make big sales."

Right, so you have some alternatives to reach an outcome of
releasing a record, but having an outcome of making a *hit* record
is not well formed.

Probably there are ways that you will find to improve the chances,
but the absolute level of sales or popularity isn't going to be in
your control. We should also note that it is Amanada's outcome to
make a hit record, but that she needs to work with the band to
achieve it. You need to make sure that you all have the same outcome, and are all following through the various paths that you
might need to get there.

OK, finish writing out and checking those outcomes over the next
week. Once you have written a final version of all three, including
timetables, put it somewhere that you will see it regularly, to check
how well you are getting on with achieving the goals.

Now we can apply this to communicating. First we need some sort
of outcome or desired state, for you and for the other person. You
will have to work out what you positively want; how you are
going to achieve it; and why you want it. This we contrast with
what is happening now, the present state. Then you must decide
what to influence – the situation, behaviour, thinking or feeling –
and how you are going to make the change – by doing something,
teaching something or influencing the other person. You can then
decide the time frame, and look at it from the right angle. Make the
changes, and your communicating will improve.

What do you need to do now? You might want to review and add
to your own issues that you developed in Exercises 1.1 and 1.6.
Consider them in terms of situation, behaviour, thoughts and feelings. Look at them from other people's viewpoints and from
different parts of your time line. Then you can develop outcomes
to improve them. Keep working on those outcomes – how many
will you have achieved by the time we meet again? What else
might you want well-formed outcomes for?

Just think what you can achieve for yourself before we meet again. Try using the self-pacing technique before important conversations to get yourself into a good state. And you can use the Meta-mirror to prepare for what the other person will say. How much easier will just those two techniques make your communicating?

Day Two:
Making Their
Moves

Welcome back. Last time, we looked at some aspects of communication, and at structuring issues and outcomes. I hope you have learned some useful tips about good states for starting a conversation, and some new ways of perceiving others. In this section, we are going to learn some more useful techniques.

● *Communicating*

We are going to start by outlining the structure of communicating with another person. This has three stages: *Matching*, *Pacing* and *Leading*. Matching is getting in touch with the person you want to speak to and drawing some response from him or her. Pacing involves getting information from them to enable you to know what the person wants and values, and how he or she processes information. Leading is putting your message across in terms that the other person will understand, appreciate and value.

The remaining topics for today are about matching physiology and behaviour. How you look and sound to another person will influence how they respond to you. You will find that you can talk to someone who looks and sounds like you more easily than someone 'odd'. Physiology includes the way you are sitting or standing, your expression and breathing patterns. It also includes the tone of voice that you use. Behaviour includes unconscious movements and tics as well as things that you are aware of doing.

● *Rapport*

Rapport is the art of including other people. It is an attitude that includes being aware of them as individuals, listening to what they are saying and observing what they are doing. The most important thing is that you respond – in word and deed – appropriately. You will learn to interpret what people are saying in order to appreciate what it means to them, and phrase what you want to say in their terms. In this session, we are concentrating on the physiology and behaviour of rapport.

A quick way of gaining rapport is to feed back to the other person exactly what you see and hear from them. We will learn how powerful this is, and find out that matching physiology and behaviour is much more important than matching words.

• *Calibrating*

If we can copy someone else's physiology and behaviour, we can also get information from what we see and hear. Some signs are conventional – nodding in agreement, laughing at a joke and shouting in alarm. You will learn to interpret a wider range of signs, particularly about truth and lying, and be aware of their nuances.

On the topic of appearance, Paul has a point that arose out of the outcome-setting exercise last time. Can you tell us how you made your outcome well formed and what you achieved?

> "Hi. I'm wearing all my flashiest brand names today. And that was what my outcome was about. Normally, I have to dress very conservatively for work – dark suit, white shirt, that sort of thing. I like smart clothes, but I'd got out of the habit of buying them. So I set myself an outcome of buying a set of clothes for this week's seminar, clothes that I'd feel great wearing, and you'd be able see how good I look. I set myself a budget that I could afford, and took three hours off to buy the clothes. Obviously I knew what to do and when, and the process went smoothly. From an ecology point of view, I knew that I would feel better and that other people would view me more positively: that checks out because I sat here last time and didn't speak, and today I'm the first contributor."

That certainly sounds like an achievement. Those of you who have tried to achieve a well-formed outcome and not yet succeeded might like to choose a simple example like this to start with.

Communicating

Every conversation has three stages. First, you have to get in touch with the person that you want to talk to. This may be a technical process, such as telephoning them, or shouting to attract their attention. This hasn't really started the conversation, though. Unless the person is prepared to hear what you have to say, you are not communicating. You need to achieve *rapport*. Both of you have to agree to include the other. This stage in communicating is called *matching*. As we shall find out over the next three sessions, you can achieve matching in terms of physiology and behaviour, thought and language, and feelings and values. Initially, though, physiological matching is the most powerful way of establishing rapport.

The next stage of communicating is *pacing*. This is the information-gathering stage. You find out how the other person behaves and reacts in various situations, how they use language, something about what they know and believe, and what they value. You also learn about the emotional content of the situation. We will cover these aspects of communication on days four, five and six.

The final stage of communicating is *leading*. This is where you put across what you want from the conversation. You may be trying to get the other person to do something, learn something, or value something. Your outcome might be to deepen a friendship, get a subordinate to carry out orders, influence your boss, teach a class or sell something. By putting your message in the terms that are most likely to be understood and appreciated – the ones that you have found by pacing – you stand the best chance of achieving your outcome. The last three days of the course are dedicated to leading.

Rapport

Today we are going to work on all aspects of getting in touch. This is the first requirement if we are going to communicate. If you want to be in a conversation, you need to listen to the other person, and know that he or she is listening to you. You need to develop what is known as *rapport*. It is part of a process of feeding back interest, or *matching*. If you are writing to someone, or speaking to a large group, you will have to motivate them. This will involve getting to know something about them so that you can feed it back to show you are interested in them. We will call this *pacing*. Only then can you add in your own information or try to get them to do something. This is the process of *leading*.

In this section, we will study the behavioural aspects of matching: making some sense of what people do. The theory of matching is that the more similar you are, the better you will communicate. The techniques we will cover in this module are physical matching and calibration.

Starting a conversation can be very difficult for some people. If you don't start properly, you may not be able to communicate very well. With a little understanding and patience, the effect of the communication can be significantly improved. You need to start a good conversation by getting in touch with yourself. Be happy with the situation. We'll start by all doing the self-pacing exercise from Day One to put us in a good state. Please do that now.

Before we communicate, we need an outcome. To put it crudely, you need to have a reason to talk to the other person, a strategy for getting your point across, and an idea of what you want to tell them. You also need to know when you have done all that is useful, have a strategy for ending the conversation and a reason for moving on. You should also bear in mind that you may not be the one starting the conversation, and that the other person will have their own reasons, strategies and points to get across.

Turn to Handout 2.1. It shows some of the Whizzitts salespeople in meetings. Have you ever really noticed people in conversation? That even when you are out of earshot, you can tell whether the meeting is a success or not? In the first scene, Jo is on the left and the client is on the right. Jo looks very agitated, while the client is very steady in his chair. In this second picture, Bill is sitting on the left, looking calm and languid, while the client is leaning forward, very agitated and slapping papers on his desk. In the third one, the client is sitting to the left of Dave. You can see that they are both sitting in the same sort of way and looking at each other, but they have different expressions. Finally, Diane is with another client, walking through a car park, keeping pace with each other, almost hand in hand – yes, they turn simultaneously and shake hands.

Let's pretend we are in a club. There is a stand-up comic on stage. Most of the audience is laughing and clapping. Some of the audience members are standing up, with their backs to the action.

Now we have a mime artist on the stage . He is going to take up a number of poses. What do you think he is intending to portray in each scene? In the first one he is seated. His head and arms hang down. His face is slack and his eyes are pretty well shut. There is very little movement. Now a second one: he is more upright, with his hand supporting his chin. He seems to be gazing into the distance, although his eyes are moving about. Have you got all that?

Why are we learning to pace others?

Matching

There are a number of presuppositions or working hypotheses in NLP. These are unproven but useful descriptions of the interaction between the mind, body and world. The chief of these is *"The map is not the territory"*, that is, that any theory, map or model we make of reality is going to be wrong. It will at least be incomplete, because we cannot describe everything about even a single object in a finite time. It is also likely to contain errors or distortions because we have ignored (or do not know of) certain things, misinterpreted evidence, jumped to conclusions or simplified in misleading ways. What it also means is that the map anyone else makes is also wrong, and extremely likely to differ from our map.

Communicating is a process of adding something from our map to that of someone else. In order to add to their map, we need to know a certain amount about it. Most immediately, we have to know something about the form and style in which that person represents their map. If we present our additions in a radically different layout, people seem to have great difficulty fitting the new piece in – they may not even realise that it is something that would form a useful part of their map. For example, we might give someone some useful verbal instructions: "Go to the counter and you will be given £500." However, if we give these instructions in English, and the other person only has the Yoruba language in their map of the world, they will not be interpreted as useful.

Handout 2.1: The Sales Experience

Sketch 1: Jo with a Client

Sketch 2: Bill with a Client

Sketch 3: Dave with a Client

Sketch 4: Diane with a Client

This could apply at less obvious levels: gestures may not be universally understood, or voice tones that are meant to suggest helpfulness might be heard as threatening. We don't even all drive on the same side of the road. Failing to miss more subtle personal or cultural differences may not cause complete failure of the communication, but they may add distortions, or make it less likely that the recipient believes what they are being told.

There is evidence that the internal forms of the map, such as information storage and retrieval, beliefs and values, are reflected by external behaviours, whether physiology, action, or use of language. This may not always be true, since we are capable of acting and lying – if we could not, we would have no way of adjusting to the form and style of others. Nevertheless, the acting and lying are part of our map of the world.

Matching is the process of reflecting behaviour and language back to the other person.

The theory of matching suggests that this is the best way to get our ideas added to their map, and so communicate. We will try this out in practice. Even if the other person is acting or lying, matching their behaviour and language stills allows us access to their map. Today, we are concentrating on the *behavioural* aspects of this reflection; over the next two days we will cover beliefs and values, which can also be reflected back.

So, we'll go back to the mime artist. What was he trying to portray in the last section? Taking the idea of the map and territory not being identical, we cannot *know* exactly what he intended, but what do you think? What does the hunched, slack position mean to you? Is he happy and active? That interpretation is not in my map. Colloquially, we say someone is *down*, so is that a physical reflection of it? How do you interpret the pose with his chin in his hand, looking into infinity? Is he active or passive? Is he talking to someone else, or possibly to himself? Is he showing any emotion? Now remember being in the comedy club. Who is getting the message – someone who already knows it all, and knows how to act, or someone who is still processing it and doing something different? What communication is happening between members of the audience?

Let's go back to the sketches. Who do you think made the biggest sale?

If you are communicating well, you naturally move into a joint space, where you will move together, share expressions, voice tone, language and emotions. This is called *rapport*.

Rapport is a state of mind, in which you accept and work within the reality of the other person, so far as you can understand it. There will be things that seem wrong to you. They don't fit your view of the world. And there will be things in it that seem wrong to the other person, because you have misinterpreted the information that they have given you. Any errors or misunderstanding can, however, act as *feedback* information, and you can make adjustments to the message, calibrating the other person's reaction. Remember that this is not just a one-way process. The other people in the system will also be trying to communicate. They may be matching and calibrating you.

We will start by learning ways of *matching* to get closer to other people, so that they will stay with what you are communicating. You should remain aware that you have the choice to break off the process when you need to – what we shall call *mismatching*.

The theory of physiological *matching* is that by matching the *external appearance and behaviours* of the person you are communicating with you will take on some of their inner states, and thus be closer to their internal map: this then allows improved communicating. It has been estimated that a large part of the message is lost if the *physiological cues* are missing. The most important physiological cues seem to be posture, expression, breathing and voice tonality, and it is those that we will practise matching.

Just imagine that you are in a pub or a restaurant. It's a scene you see all the time. A couple at a table near you are completely caught up with each other. They sit facing each other, and they have taken up the same posture; they have their hands in similar positions; they raise their cups at the same time. They are not speaking. Then suddenly they both smile. If you look closely, their breathing is in step. They are sharing an experience, and communicating powerfully.

I'm going to set up the exercises so that you can do them here, and repeat them whenever you can find somebody to work with you on them: you want to practise these techniques until they become automatic.

Exercise 2.1: Noticing Others

Turn to face some people near you, and just observe their posture. Are they sitting upright, leaning forward, back or sideways? Where are their hands and feet? How do they hold their heads? Look at their faces. Take in the way they hold their muscles, especially round the eyes and mouth.

Now look at one person's movements and gestures. These may show up more when he or she is talking to someone else. See what is happening – blinks, nods, waves and twitches – and get a feeling for the rhythms and patterns that these set up. Find the clues about the other person's breathing. Maybe you can see the rise and fall of the chest, to show you the rate of breathing. Which part of the chest is he or she breathing from? Some other cues may be the cheeks moving in and out, the opening of the mouth or the flaring of nostrils.

Harry, would you like to tell us what else you noticed?

"I can pick up rhythms of movement. Oh, yes, the patterns of speech also help you to mark the breathing – most people can only speak on the out-breath!"

At home, you can practise observing this on the TV – choose your favourite news-reader, chat-show host, pundit or whoever, and get into the habit of noticing posture, expressions and gestures. Watch how your model breathes and how the breathing changes.

Now, what else have you noticed? That you were starting to mimic the elements that you were noticing? This is a normal reaction, showing a natural desire to get closer to the state of, or understand, the person we are concentrating on. Let's not fight that, but go with it.

Voice tone is also important. Have you ever noticed that there are some people who get through to you more easily than others do? You remember the messages they give you. Others either put you off listening at all, or you rapidly forget what they have said.

The elements which can be important are pitch – how high or low the voice sounds; pace – how quickly or slowly the words come out; and volume. Accent is often a combination of all three of these, together with the pattern of tonal shifts within the sentence – how questions, phrases and punctuation are marked, and which words are emphasised, shortened or slurred together. As with the other physiological states, we are most receptive when the other person is using voice tones that are similar to ours. With voice tones, we are unlikely to be able to match exactly the pitch, pace, volume and accent that someone else is using. If you are a soprano and he is a bass, all you can do is move your tonality down a little, to indicate a shift towards them. Similarly, you can hint at, rather than match exactly, big differences in loudness, speed of delivery and tonal shifts. You can practise listening to voice tones on the radio, and repeat what is being said using voice tones as near the original as possible. It doesn't matter if what you are saying is nonsense, you are just aiming to match the speech patterns.

Exercise 2.2: Physiological Matching

For this exercise, it is best to work in threes: a Model, a Matcher and an Observer.

Decide who is going to match first and who is going to model. These two should sit facing each other, about four feet apart. The Observer can move around to help the Matcher.

The Model should sit naturally, and talk about something casually. The Matcher should start with posture – notice how the Model is sitting: feet, legs, back, head, arms, hands. If the Observer can see any differences, just help the Matcher to get into position.

Now the Matcher should become aware of the expression on the Model's face and copy that, and become aware of the kind of gestures that are being made – head movements, hand waving, any tics – and their tempo and rhythm. You don't have to match those gestures in kind – you might tap your knee, rather than nod, for example – but match the pattern of rhythm and tempo.

As you become aware of the Model's natural body rhythm, the breathing pattern should become easier to note. Just as a start, though, the Model might indicate with a hand where on the chest the breathing is centred. Move the hand in and out to demonstrate the in- and out-breaths. Then go back to a natural state.

Once the Matcher has taken on the Model's breathing pattern, it is time to think about voice tones. To make it easier, the Model should speak a short sentence. Then on the next out-breath, the Matcher should repeat the sentence using voice tones as similar to those of the model as is comfortable. After three or four sentences, the Observer can start to coach the Matcher to reduce the differences that they perceive. Go on until you are all comfortable with the match.

The exercise should take about 10 to 15 minutes. Then change round, with the Matcher becoming the new Observer, the Observer becoming the new Model and the Model becoming the new Matcher. Repeat the whole process so that you all have a go in each role.

OK, how was that? What did it feel like to be matching the other person? You noticed how difficult it was, in some cases, to break away from doing the exercise. You were so deeply into it that time was unimportant. You had real rapport. And you will get better at this the more you practise, so find colleagues at work, members of your family or friends, teach them the process, and then work on it together. Judging by the expressions, this practice won't be any hardship.

We did notice, though, that breaking away from rapport could be difficult. There may be good reasons to end this kind of contact. You could have completed your business. Maybe you don't want to buy another lawn mower, or become an apostle of the new church on the block. Perhaps you have an urgent appointment. Or you don't really want to spend the whole night talking to your friendly neighbourhood mugger.

To end the rapport, we reverse the process. Instead of matching, we mismatch. Break eye contact, adopt a different posture, change the expression, gestures and breathing pattern you are using. Change your voice tones. Disagree. And move away.

We'll do a series of three exercises to show which are the most important elements in mismatching for you.

Exercise 2.3a: Mismatching Words
Get into pairs, Model and Matcher. For the first part of the exercise, the Model will talk about any subject she or he is comfortable with. For three minutes, the Matcher will *match* physiologically and *agree* with the Model and reinforce what they are saying.

Then I'll ring the bell, and the Matcher should continue the physiological rapport, but *disagree* with and challenge what is being said. I'll let that go on for a minute or so, then ring the bell again.

The Matcher should go back to *agreeing*, and continue the physiological matching. Then when I ring the bell twice, change over roles, and we'll go through the exercise again for the new Model and Matcher.

That seems to have been difficult for most people – it was a struggle to disagree while staying in rapport. Did anyone find it easy? Yes, Paul – did you get into a good state of rapport? No, I thought not. It may be a stretch, but as you practise, you will find it easier, even where you don't have a lot in common. How did that feel to the Models? A bit strange, with the disagreements sounding rather forced? It's not a very natural way of behaving, is it?

Exercise 2.3b: Mismatching the Body

Get back into your pairs, Model and Matcher. For the first part of this exercise, the Model will again talk about any subject he or she is comfortable with. For three minutes, the Matcher will *match* physiologically and *agree* with the Model, and reinforce what they are saying.

This time, when I ring the bell, start *mismatching* physiologically, but keep *agreeing* verbally. I'll let that go on for a minute or so, then ring the bell again. Then the Matcher should go back to matching fully.

Then when I ring the bell twice, change over roles, and we'll go through the exercise again for the new Model and Matcher.

That seems to have been easier to do. In the middle, when you were mismatching, did you feel committed to your agreement, or were you just going through the motions? If the Model had been trying to sell you something you didn't want, would you have been able to walk away? And the Models – how did you feel when you were being mismatched? Was it very uncomfortable? Did you want to leave the conversation as well?

Exercise 2.3c: Mismatching the Voice

Right, let's find out how this could work on the *telephone*. Find a new partner for this exercise, and work as Model and Matcher. Put your chairs back-to-back, so that you can hear but not see the person you are working with.

The Model will start a conversation again, and the Matcher will *match* the voice tones – pitch, pace, volume and accent tonality, while *agreeing* with the content. You should also be able to move some way towards matching the breathing, after the practice you've already had.

On the first bell, the Matcher will continue to *match* the voice tone, but *disagree* with the content, for a minute or so.

When the bell rings a second time, return to *agreeing* with the Model.

After the third bell, continue to *agree* with the content, but *mismatch* the voice tones – go deeper or shriller, faster or slower, louder or more quiet – or change the accent stresses: I'll give you another minute or so on that.

Lastly, on the fourth bell, go back to a tonal *match* and *agreement*. Then, as usual, change roles and we'll repeat the exercise.

So, does rapport work on the phone as well? You were only mismatching the voice tones, but it still had a profound effect, far more than disagreeing with the content. And just notice how quickly you can now match the voice tones. With a little more practice, it should become automatic, when you want to do it – and mismatching will also become automatic when you need that.

I have suggested that you find some opportunities to practise these matching skills at work, at home or with your friends by briefing someone to be your Model (and by letting them model you). I strongly recommend doing a little self-pacing first. When you are confident, you can start using the skills in normal conversations. These might be informal, in the office or the pub, or they might be phone calls to friends or relatives. Don't try too hard at first – just allow yourself to move towards matching when it seems appropriate. If it is too obvious, the other person may start to concentrate on why you are acting like that, rather than on what you are saying. Aim to make these rapport techniques part of your normal behaviour.

Calibrating

Let's now look at this from the second position – the viewpoint of the person you are talking to. How do you know you have their attention? And how do you know anything else about them? The only senses we can normally use to find out about someone else are *seeing* and *hearing*. In intimate and special circumstances (e.g. when shaking hands), we may get additional information through *touching* or smelling another person, but our eyes and ears are our only long-range intelligence systems. If we have some limitations in what we can sense, for example when we are on the phone, we will have to emphasise the other ones.

We can see the kinds of information that we were using in order to build rapport in Exercise 2.2 – posture, gestures, expressions, breathing, skin colours and muscle tones. We can hear tonalities of their voice, and the information that they choose to give us in language. The question is how we interpret the information that we are sensing. Thus any conclusions that we draw from what we see or hear should be regarded as "mind-reading" until we have a chance to prove them.

Let's see what is possible. Please get into the right state by pacing yourself (Exercise 1.2) again.

Exercise 2.4: Visual Calibration

Work in pairs, as Model and Calibrator. You can stand or sit facing your partner. The Model should take a coin and hold it in one hand, visible to the Calibrator. The Model should try to stay in the same state throughout the exercise.

The Calibrator will ask, "Is the coin in your left hand?" and the Model will answer, "Yes". The Calibrator knows whether this is a lie or the truth. Then the Calibrator will ask, "Is the coin in your right hand?" and the Model will answer, "Yes". The Calibrator will notice the differences in the Model's physiology – they may show up in posture, gestures, expression, breathing, facial colour or muscle tone. The Calibrator should ask the Model about the coin until the truth and lying states are obvious.

Then the Model should conceal the coin in one fist. The Calibrator will ask, "Is the coin in your left hand?" and the Model will answer, "Yes". The Calibrator will then say whether the Model is telling the truth or lying. If you are wrong, then calibrate the states again; otherwise continue until you are right three times in a row.

After that switch round so that the Model becomes the Calibrator. Repeat the whole exercise. You shouldn't need more than about five minutes each.

Good – that was easy, wasn't it? Many of you experimented by telling the Model what signs they were giving, and getting them to try to keep a "poker face" – and you could still tell when they were lying.

So, how else could we use this type of calibration? We are looking for changes, so we need two or more states that we can get information about from the other person in order to differentiate them. You might try calibrating the guests in TV game shows such as *Call My Bluff*, where one panellist out of three is telling the truth and the other two are lying. You can make the exercise easier by turning off the sound to reduce the distraction.

Another exercise you could try with your partner or a friend is seeing how they react to people they like. Ask them to think of someone they like and someone they are neutral towards. Get the names. You say the name, and they think of the person. Calibrate the differences you can see. Then ask them to think of someone else, and you tell them how strongly they like that person.

At the office, you might just notice how your colleagues look and behave when they are talking about particular people and things that they like, hate, fear... Search for patterns, and keep checking. In a sales situation, you might mention a list of things that most people will react favourably towards, and some that they will dislike, and calibrate the client. Then, when you talk about something important to the sale, you will be able to calibrate whether the customer is happy with it or not.

Exercise 2.5: Auditory Calibration

Are we ready for another exercise? This one is just to calibrate voice tones, as if you were making a phone call. Get into pairs, Model and Calibrator.

Sit back to back, so that you can hear but not see or touch the other person. The Model should think of someone that they are impressed by, and say who it is. Then, thinking of that person, count out loud from one to twenty. Then the Model should think of someone they are definitely not impressed by, and say who it is. Then, thinking of that person, count out loud from one to twenty.

The Calibrator can ask the model to repeat this to pick up the differences in pace, volume and voice pitch.

Then the Calibrator should ask the Model to think of one of the people and count out loud from one to twenty. The Calibrator should give the name. If you are wrong, recalibrate the Model. Go on until you get three correct in a row. Once the first person has managed to calibrate, switch over roles. Repeat the exercise for the new Model. Take about five minutes each for this exercise.

Yes, good. A bit more difficult this time – most of us are more used to looking for differences than to listening for them. The cues can be quite subtle – a slight quickening or slowing, a change of emphasis or tone. It is well worth practising this with a few different people, getting used to hearing the voice tones rather than just the content of what is being said.

It might be worth working with your partner or a friend on the phone. Calibrate the differences in voice tone between what is important, good/bad and so on. Then you can both be alerted to the tonal value of the message even when you are telling 'white lies'.

You could practise with *Call My Bluff*, again. This time, cover the screen, and calibrate whether the guests are lying from their voice tones alone.

Exercise 2.6: Coin Dropping
Here's something you could use as a party game. Everyone gets up and stands in a circle. Get a handful of different coins. Have someone name them, one at a time, and then drop them onto a hard surface. Then you turn around, or cover your eyes. Ask the person to drop the coins again, and you name them. Practise until you can get them all right.

Perhaps you can think of situations where you might prefer to calibrate by touch or smell rather than sight or sound! Why not try it and find out how useful it can be?

Today we have learned about matching behaviour, especially gaining rapport and calibrating others. We have seen how power-ful physiological rapport is in gaining agreement. You have also discovered that people's moods show up in their bodies and that you can tell if they are lying just from their expressions or voice tones. So now, go out and practise and find out how else you can use your rapport and calibration skills.

Day Three:
Hearing Their Words

Let's just remind ourselves of the purpose of this course. You want to improve your communicating, and you have set some outcomes for doing that. Keep those in mind, as we go on to see how we can match the thinking processes of the person we are talking to. Specifically, we are going to consider the words that they say.

Let's start by previewing today's topics.

• *The Structure of Learning*
Learning is a process that takes us from not knowing that we don't know something, through awareness, to a point where we only realise that we know it if someone asks us.

• *Congruence*
Is the person you are talking to reinforcing what they are saying with their body language? Is she saying "yes" and shaking her head? Is he smiling or wincing when he says "thank you"? Signals of congruence can help you decide what is really going on.

• *Verbal Predicates*
Some of us *see* the world about us. Some people *hear* what is going on. Others need to *feel* what is right. There are different ways of accessing information, and our preferred channel shows up in the words we use to describe the world. If you talk to someone in their own language, using their verbal predicates, you stand the best chance of getting through to them.

• *Clean Language*
The questions we ask can lead to us getting a particular answer. To get information about another person we need to take care to use language patterns that avoid making assumptions.

• *Presuppositions*
Everything we say is incomplete. The listener is forced to read between the lines in order to make sense of what we are saying. Your completion of the sense may not be the same as mine. If I say, "She hit me", I might mean that Susan dealt me another card, while you might think that my mother slapped me. Presuppositions need to be tested in order to avoid error. That last sentence is a presupposition.

The Structure of Learning

I hope that you have found some time since the last seminar to practise some of the techniques we learned. One resource that is always scarce is time: time to think about the outcomes as well as achieve them. Sir John, as Chairman of Whizzitts, you must be as busy as anybody is?

> "I am, but I'm also fairly organised. My secretary has orders to leave a gap in my diary every day so that I have some time for myself – to get my thoughts in order. I have found the self-pacing exercise a useful way of starting that daily period of reflection. I have also started noticing people more – what exactly they are doing, and what it might mean to me."

After talking to some of you over coffee, I think that's quite a common reaction. And it seems that you are beginning to match people you are speaking to without being too self-conscious about it. In fact, it is becoming automatic.

Let's have a story about how I learned to drive. Before we learn a skill, we don't know the details of what we can't do. I had seen my parents driving, so I knew that it involved wiggling a wheel and pushing and pulling at various pedals, switches and levers. I assumed that because other people can drive, all I had to do was get in the car and speed away. This is called *unconscious incompetence*.

Once I was behind the wheel, I started to learn a little and panic a lot. Nothing seemed to work properly. The engine kept stalling. The car would leap about on the road. Traffic came from nowhere. There was so much to remember – push down the clutch *before* trying to change gear. I thought that I would never put it all together. This is the longest stage in any learning – at least, it seems so at the time. It got worse, because the more I learned, the more aware I became of the range of things that I could not do. This is the stage of *conscious incompetence*.

Then, gradually, I began to realise that I could do some of the techniques. As long as I talked myself through it – mirror, signal, engage first gear, handbrake off, clutch out and accelerate away –

"Once I was behind the wheel, I started to learn a little and panic a lot."

I could start moving the car without a kangaroo hop. This isn't an easy phase, and there were plenty of opportunities for me to show a lack of skill. Still, eventually I started getting some of the rewards, like a driving licence. This degree of learning is called *conscious competence*.

As I continued to practise, the skills become automatic, and I no longer had to think about how to turn the wheel or change gear. I could drive and listen to the radio, or talk to my passengers. I would arrive at my destination without being aware of how many times I had changed gear or turned on the indicators. I had become *unconsciously competent*. That isn't quite the final stage, however. It may be important to know what we are doing or have just done. We can become *aware of competence*. As a result of continued practice we can develop further skills. A skilled police driver can drive and talk through what he is seeing and doing – my driving isn't that skilled. I can, however, set myself to remember the important points of *how* everyone was speaking in a meeting where I also have to consciously record the content of *what* they are saying.

Remember that you can keep practising until you are unconsciously competent in these techniques for communicating. Then you can use them without thinking about it, unless you need to.

Congruence

One thing that came up in conversation this morning was that some of you noticed that what you were calibrating from people's expressions didn't always match their words. Last week we were calibrating for lying, and noticed changes in expression, posture, gestures and breathing. This is just a special case of *incongruity*, where body language and words do not match. We can find incongruity happening *simultaneously*. You might say, "Yes, dear", and shake your head at the same time. Oh, yes, that seems to be quite a common experience. We can also find it happening *sequentially* – someone says, "Of course I'd like to do that", and then grimaces. I can see that some of you have experience of that one as well. You can also be incongruous in matching someone else. The person expects a particular response and gets something different, even though you are agreeing.

We have worked on congruous behaviours – matching – and now we want to practise congruity in language.

We all use words, every day, to communicate with our work colleagues, customers, family or friends. Just think of some occasions where you have failed to get the result you wanted by using the wrong words, or where you could have got a better result if the words had been more suited to the person you were talking to. Maybe you have offended someone, or driven that person away. Someone may have changed the subject from the one you wanted to talk about. Or if the other person was obliged to stay with you, he or she might have looked bored, or not taken in what you were saying.

> ### Exercise 3.1: Using the Right Words
> Get out a piece of paper and write down at least five examples where the language you were using got a reaction that you weren't expecting.

Now get together in small groups to discuss your examples and look for some patterns. We'll join in with Harry, Amananda and Vanessa.

Amanada: "Most of my examples are about saying the wrong thing at the wrong time – I see myself breaking the mood, giving away secrets, changing the viewpoint when others were interested in it. That's all to do with not matching and pacing. I hadn't really got into conversation with them, I was just trying to get their attention and put my point across without listening to what was going on."

Harry: "I'm a bit the opposite. I'll listen, but I don't find the right moment to get my points in. I end up just agreeing, or getting bored and frustrated. And if I do say anything, people don't seem to want to listen to what I have to say."

Vanessa: "I've got a specific example – I was talking to a couple of friends about my holiday in Peru. I wanted to share the experience of swimming in the sea, and the feel of walking from a hot, sunny street into the cool of an ancient church, but they only seemed to be interested in the views, and the photographs I could have taken."

Amanada: "Oh, I saw a wonderful film on the TV about Peru..."

Harry: "Yes, I heard about that – the traditional music, the sounds of the markets..."

Vanessa: "It's happening again! You had to be there to experience it..."

Come back together. I think those discussions will give us quite a lot to work on. Even though most of you were in reasonable physiological rapport during that exercise, the communicating was getting quite difficult at times. You didn't all seem to be on the same wavelength, did you?

It's time to talk about some of the difficulties that are arising from poor communicating in Whizzitts Ltd. Let's just take a hypothetical management meeting between Vanessa, Apricot and PS. PS wants a stand at a trade fair, so Vanessa will be recruiting some temporary support staff and Apricot should provide the leaflets and displays. The fair starts next week and the arrangements are still not complete. Can the three of you sit here at the front of the room and have that meeting, so that we can all share?

PS: "The clock is ticking, but you still haven't told me you'll be ready, either of you. I don't like the sound of that. Vanessa, I want you to tell me that you have four people to greet the customers on Monday. Apricot, let me hear that your department is tuned up and that the new literature will ring bells for us."

Vanessa: "Everything is solid, and we'll do what has to be done. There are two more bodies to interview, and I get a good feeling about them. I'm sure they'll fit in, as long as you make them comfortable."

Apricot: "You will be able to see the material tomorrow. I'm very pleased with how it looks – and the posters will really shine out. Keep everything in perspective, and we'll make a great showing. The display will make clear the depth of our commitment. Everything will be colour coordinated – based on the corporate green, of course, with different shades and textures. Pictures in colour and sketches in black and white. The whole thing will have a three-dimensional effect to draw the customers in."

Vanessa: "And good staff will add the final touches. I know it will be a weight off your mind when you see them roll up. I hope they make the right impression – warm and smooth enough to pull in the clients, but with enough gravitas to uphold the company standards."

PS: "I hear what you say, but I won't be shouting about it until I hear the rustle of money. We must get the tone and the tempo right to get the volume of referrals we need to call it a success. I hope your staff will be in good voice, and sound note-takers."

My thanks go to the three of you. Can I ask everyone else, which one of them convinced you that they knew their job the best? We'll have a simple show of hands. Who thought that PS was the soundest? Just one, and that a bit dubious. Who is supporting Vanessa? That's two or three. And who sees Apricot as best? She has four or five. And the others weren't really talking your language, or seeing things your way, or were out of touch?

Most people assume that the way they do things, the language they use, and the values they have are the best, the most obvious, natural, the only ones. These are *presuppositions*. And like all presuppositions, they may be useful, or they may be wrong.

Verbal Predicates

We talked a little bit about how we sense the world last time. We can only get information by seeing, hearing sounds, touching, smelling, tasting or having someone else describe it. Any experience, memory or processing of information has to be done through one or more of these six channels: **V**isual (sights); **A**uditory (sounds); **K**inaesthetic (physical feelings); **O**lfactory (odours); **G**ustatory (tastes); and **D**igital (words). Thus, if you are eating a meal, you might **[V]** see the food on the table and the other people sitting round you; **[A]** hear the clink of cutlery and the buzz of conversation; **[K]** feel the knife and fork in your hands; **[O]** smell the rich aroma of chocolate; **[G]** taste the acidity of lemon; **[D]** be aware of the conversation. In NLP terms, this is called the *6-tuple* of the experience **[VAKOGD]**. In many cases, smell and taste are relatively unimportant, and can be treated as part of the kinaesthetic, giving a *4-tuple* description **[VAKD]**.

Each experience, memory, or process of analysis may include all the elements of the 4-tuple, but with differing emphasis and order. Nevertheless, for similar types of experiences, we tend to have a pattern of which element is accessed first, and which is the most important. Consciously, we can only process one element at a time, although we will be aware of all of them.

The patterns that we most regularly use will show up in our use of language. The markers are the descriptive words that we use, called *verbal predicates*. Most people show a clear preference for one of the four sets of predicates, and may be described as Visual, Auditory, Kinaesthetic or Digital. The set that you most often use in a particular situation is called your *primary predicate system*.

Handout 3.1 shows a list of the types of words that are typically used when people have particular elements of the 4-tuple leading their description of a scene or memory. There is also a list of words that are ambiguous, and could be part of more than one lead system. This is by no means a complete list, more a guide as to what to look for.

Handout 3.1: Examples of Verbal Predicates

Visual	Auditory	Kinaesthetic	Digital
see	hear	feel	know
look	sound	touch	realise
glance	whisper	brush	hint
flash	murmur	click	sudden
glow	hum	tickle	occasional
twinkle	whistle	itch	communication
glare	rumble	spread	detail
stare	noise	rub	location
vision	tempo	quake	duration
colour	pitch	pressure	frequency
perspective	shout	texture	intensity
size	ring/bell	temperature	dimensions
contrast	call	moisture	importance
motion	quiet	taste [G]	compare
space	hear	aroma [O]	calculate
watch	listen	empty	vacant
view	in key	weigh	compute
brilliant	dissonant	hitting the spot	satisfied
flickering	song	painful	unpleasant
film	thunder	movie	theatre
lightning	trill	strike	trouble
bright	loud	lively	effective
black	scream	walk	education
white	laugh	jump	health
read	melody	fly	business
sketch	voice	try-out	attempt
picture	hail	build	art
vanish	call	break	signal
fade	toll	flow	communicate
ray	ultrasound	toil	detail
laser		cut	prepare

Ambiguous

light [V/K]	dull [V/K]	smart [V/K]	tone [V/A]
shape [V/K]	sharp [A/K]	flat [All]	soar [A/K]
scale [All]	range [All]	place [V/K]	range [V/A]
clash [A/K]	bang [A/K]	fire [V/K]	wave [A/K]
score [A/K]	play [A/K]	bubble [A/K]	soft [A/K]
low [All]	high [All]	model [V/K]	draw [V/K]
face [V/K]	back [V/K]	front [V/K]	form [All]
figure [All]	flag [V/K]	round [All]	point [V/K]
pause [A/K]	top [All]	tonic [A/K]	tape [V/A]

Exercise 3.2: Finding Your Lead System

Get together in threes. One person should speak about something they like for three minutes, then something they dislike for three minutes. For the whole period, the other two members of the group should listen out for the predicates the speaker is using, and note on the worksheet which element of the 4-tuple they come from. Ignore the ambiguous predicates. One of the two listeners should act as timekeeper.

Then spend two minutes discussing which are the most and least favoured systems for the speaker and note them on the worksheet. If the two listeners disagree about the most and least favoured systems, or the results are close, the speaker may not have a single lead system. If the results are strikingly different for the "liked" and "disliked" subjects, then note that as well.

Repeat the process for the other two group members, and come back together in about 30 minutes from now.

So, some of you found that easier than others. It is good to *practise* looking for these predicates in what you say and in conversation with others. For yourself, get hold of a tape recorder and talk for five minutes or so – about something you enjoy or hate, about a memory or an experience, or just describe what is going on around you. Then play back the tape and *count* the predicates of each type. To spot the use of predicates by others, either tape-record them speaking, or choose a radio or television presenter and get used to finding out the type of words that they use.

Apricot, you had a question about the material that was being described. You say that Ruth's positive experience was about taking photographs, and so was very visual, and that her negative experience was about getting lost and cold on a cross-country walk, and so was all kinaesthetic. You all had a pretty free choice of what to talk about, so the lead system preferences may well show up in the choice of topic. Ruth, could you tell us about getting here this morning?

"Well, I was late getting up. I had to rush, which I don't like. Once I was on the train, I realised it was a beautiful sunny morning, and appreciated the colours of fields and the buildings as they flickered past the window. As I came out of the station, I tripped on a paving stone and banged my knee..."

Thank you, Ruth. Did you all notice that all the negative predicates were Kinaesthetic – late getting up, rush, tripped, banged my knee – and positive language was Visual – beautiful sunny morning, appreciated the colours? Nothing Auditory even though there was plenty of opportunity to mention what she had heard. So she has two lead systems, one for positive and one for negative experiences. You may find other people who have different preferred systems for business, family and social occasions. Always bear in mind that contexts are important for any kind of communication, and that you may need to use different kinds of language in different situations.

Some of you, I notice, find it easy to track conversations for verbal predicates. It may already have become an unconscious learning. With more practice, it certainly will. Just consider when it would be appropriate just to listen to someone speaking and pick out their predicates – it can be any sort of public speaker, whether live or on the radio or television. Practise listening for predicates – and listen for the content at the same time.

Exercise 3.3 Matching Verbal Predicates

Let's find out how much better we can communicate when we match the verbal predicates of the person we are speaking to. I think it's time to start using this in a business context. Please think of a real situation where you can give business advice, or where you want to make a sale, and write down a few notes on paper.

Get into pairs. One will be the Client, and one the Advisor (or salesperson). The Advisor should brief the Client about the role to be played – the type of business, the post they hold and the situation. Make sure that the Client has enough knowledge to be able to play the role, and that he or she would be interested in the advice or the product in that situation.

Then the Client should talk about the business situation for three minutes. The Advisor should note the verbal predicates on the worksheet, and work out the Client's *lead* and *least* favoured predicate systems in this situation. If you are not sure, ask the Client to go on for a little longer.

Next, the Advisor should give the advice, or try to make the sale. For the first three minutes, use verbal predicates that match the Client's *lead* system. Then for two minutes, use verbal predicates that match the Client's *least favoured* system. Observe what happens to the Client when you start using the new predicates. Finally, spend another two minutes using verbal predicates that match the Client's *lead* system. Notice what happens to the Client when you go back to the preferred words.

Discuss what it was like using, and listening to, predicates in the lead and least preferred systems. Then change over and repeat the exercise in the opposite roles. As the new Advisor, set the scene and brief your Client.

How much more convincing was it when the Advisor used your favourite predicates? Let's have some experiences. Yes, Apricot?

"I was working with Harry, and he was role-playing a Whizzitts customer. The idea was to persuade him to take out a three-year maintenance contract. I found that his most used system is Auditory and his least favoured system is Visual. The first time we did the auditory match, I used mainly his words back to him, which worked fine. When we switched to Visual predicates, he started to look perplexed and bored: so far so good. But when we switched back to Auditory, I used my own words, and I didn't really get much feeling of rapport or interest. When we reviewed the conversation, Harry said that he didn't use a whizzer, and he couldn't get much out of the role-play."

Well, obviously the subject will have had something to do with it. Your lead system is Digital, isn't it Apricot? And you least prefer Auditory? It could be that you didn't sound very convincing. If we are going to use others' preferred predicates, we are going to have to practise making that sound natural, and have a good list of suitable words and phrases ready to drop into the conversation.

Can I suggest three ideas for homework? First, you could 'borrow' colleagues or friends and repeat the exercise a couple of times. Second, take the handout of verbal predicates, and add to it a list of words and phrases in each lead system, suitable for your business and leisure interests. Third, get your tape recorder and make four five-minute presentations, all on the same subject, one in each predicate system, using the words and phrases that you have just found. The more you practise, the quicker you will become unconsciously competent.

Clean Language

We have just found out that Harry has an Auditory lead system and that his least used predicates are Visual ones. You have found out how much easier it is to sell advice or a product to someone like Harry by using Auditory words rather than Visual ones. This is part of the process of matching.

Let's turn that round. Assume that you want to get some information from Harry, rather than sell him something. Perhaps you want him to describe a situation from memory. What do you ask him?

Remember that all communicating has to start from a base of matching. When we are trying to match someone, our aim is to avoid adding anything of our own. We are trying to get the other person's description of a scene. We want to hear it in their words, not in ours – we weren't there to witness it. There is a danger that our feelings about the situation will pollute the recall. We want to be as neutral as possible, and use *Clean Language*, as it is called.

We start by establishing rapport, using physiological matching, as we found out last week. Then, when we start to use language, one obvious matching technique is to use Harry's own words back to him. You might get the information you need spontaneously. Consider this conversation:

"I heard someone talking about me yesterday."
"So, Harry, you heard someone talking about you yesterday?"
"Yes, my boss was telling a client how quickly I had drawn
up the new contract."
*"So your boss was telling the client how quickly you had drawn up
the new contract?"*
"They were very pleased that it could be signed this week."

We might need to use words that help our partner to report the
description, not change it. If we are trying to find her primary
predicate system, it isn't much use asking her, "What do you see?"
"What can you hear?" or "What do you feel?" It is better to say:
"How would you represent that?"

It helps to ask for things that are closely tied in with what has just
been said. You could ask for more detail:
"I saw some animals."
"You saw some animals: what kind of animals were they?"
"There were three antelopes being attacked by a pair of
lions."

It might be important to know what else was there:
"I saw some animals."
"You saw some animals: what else did you see?"
"There was a cameraman and Richard Attenborough with a
tape recorder."

You might want some further details of description:
"I saw some animals."
"You saw some animals: what were they like?"
"The antelopes were tired and dusty from racing through
the bush. The lions looked rather thin and mangy."

There are similar sorts of question for things that happened near
the event, in time or in space.
"You saw some animals: then what happened?"
"You saw some animals: where were they?"
"You saw some animals: was there anyone else there?"

Don't be more specific than you have to be. The more you add to the question, the more you risk biasing the information that you are trying to get.

"I saw some animals."

"You saw some animals from the Land Rover: what kind were they?"

"No, I wasn't in the Land Rover then. The ones we saw from the car were..."

When you are asking people to remember a situation, you start by knowing very little about it. In particular, you don't yet know the context or the emotional content. If you make assumptions, you may be wrong:

"I was having words with Charlie."

"You were having words with Charlie: what was the argument about?"

"No, it wasn't an argument."

You can just refer to the conversation, the event or the situation:

"I was having words with Charlie."

"You were having words with Charlie: what was the conversation about?"

"He was blaming me for the late delivery of his order."

You might want to ask what your partner concluded or learned from the situation, so long as you are fairly sure that he or she did learn or conclude something from it. Be careful, though, that you don't suggest what that conclusion might be.

Clean Language is about exercising your listening skills. Match the words and verbal predicates of your partner, and use a minimal number of neutral phrases to seek the information that you need.

Exercise 3.4: Getting a Description

Work in pairs, as Reporter and Witness. The Witness will think of an event that you remember in detail. I suggest that the event should be something that you saw or heard that wasn't too personal. You will need to talk about it in some detail. The Reporter will be trying to get a full description of this event by asking Clean Language questions.

To make it a bit easier, we'll have a demonstration. Could we have a volunteer Witness, please? I'll be the Reporter and ask the questions. Don't worry if the details of the event are unclear, you will remember as much as you need to. Thank you, Prudence – please come out to the front. I'll talk to the group *about what I am doing* as we go along.

Now, Prudence, do you feel comfortable talking about this event? *For the group, I need to build rapport with Prudence, so I'm using some physiological matching. I also need to know that she is happy to discuss this event. If not, we won't get good information.*

> "Yes, it struck me as funny at the time, and I'm still fascinated by it."

It struck you as funny, and you are still fascinated by it? *So, we have an agreement to talk about this event. I am simply matching the words to see what she says next.*

> "Yes, I was at my aunt's house, and my young cousins were arguing about who was the best jumper."

So, you were at your aunt's house and your cousins were arguing. Was anyone else there? *I could choose a number of ways to get background detail: I have chosen to find out the 'cast list'.*

> "Just the four of us; my Aunt Jemima was out shopping. I was about 20 at the time, and the girls were all under ten. Maisie, the youngest, had just started school."

There were just the four of you. Where were you all? *Now I am trying to find out some details of the setting.*

> "Aunt Jemima had a big Victorian house near the centre of town. We were in the summer-house at the end of the garden, which has a big terrace in front of it."

You were in the summer-house at the end of the garden. What were you all doing? *We have some details of the people and place. I want to know what happened.*

"The girls had been playing on the terrace with a skipping rope. I was reading a book for the essay I had to write."

The girls had been playing on the terrace. Then what happened? *I am now trying to establish the sequence of events.*

"They came into the summer-house and asked me to judge who was the best at jumping."

They came in and asked you to be a judge. What did you do?

"I asked them what they wanted me to do. Joanne, the eldest, said that I should watch how far they could jump. And Elise wanted me to see who could jump highest."

So, Joanne wanted you to watch how far they could jump and Elise wanted you to see who could jump highest. Was there anything else? *I am interested in finding out any other details that Prudence can remember.*

"Little Maisie wanted me to judge who jumped best, rather than the longest or the highest."

So Maisie wanted you to judge who jumped *best*. What happened then?

"We all went out onto the terrace, and they jumped about for a few minutes. Then they all crowded round and asked me who was the best at jumping."

They asked you who was best at jumping. What did you say?

"I told Joanne, who was the oldest and tallest, that she had jumped further than the others, as she should have done. I told Elise, who is a natural athlete, that she had jumped higher than the others, as she should have done. And I told Maisie, who showed very little aptitude for jumping, that she could be the best jumper if she practised until she was grown up. At that point, they all started crying and shouting and hitting out at me."

Given that they all started crying and shouting and hitting out at you, have you drawn any lessons from this situation? *It seems to me that there is a point or moral of this story.*

> "Yes. It has taught me to think very carefully before putting myself in the situation of criticising or judging others, and to think what the outcome might be."

Thank you, Prudence.

So, please get together in pairs. Remember that the Reporter is responsible for creating the rapport. Ask the Witness for a general statement about the situation to start with; then follow up with Clean Language questions. You could go into a lot of detail, given enough time. Let's keep it fairly brief. Just try to get an outline of the event, so that you could write a 100-word report about it after the interview. You might want to write some notes as you go along. Take about 10 minutes, then switch roles and repeat the exercise for the new Witness.

OK, how did that go? Could all the Reporters tell us about the situations that their Witnesses observed? Most of you seem quite confident. Most people can recall a situation that they have observed in quite a lot of detail with only the most general prompting.

I heard some questioning that seemed to put up blocks in the way of letting the information come out. It does help to repeat back some of what has just been said before you lead on again. You are likely to run into trouble, though, if you say, "You watched the incident *but why* didn't you intervene?" Saying *but* or *however* just negates what the other person has said. You should avoid that sort of question, which imposes your view. Let the Witness tell it as it was. You also need to be careful about asking "Why?" This forces the Witness to stop recalling the situation and think about his or her reaction to the event. You may not be able to take them back into it. If you need to ask that sort of analytical question, it is better to wait until the description is complete.

OK, you need to practise Clean Language until it sounds normal, both to you and to the person you are questioning. You could get into the habit of asking friends or colleagues to tell you about things that have happened to them: most people are flattered to get the attention.

Presuppositions

Let's end this session by looking at a language pattern that we often ignore. That is an example of it. I have *presupposed* that we often ignore the presuppositions that are made in conversation. We'll take another example. In the sentence "John prembt Alice", the speaker presupposes that you know who John and Alice are, and that you know what *prembt* means – I don't.

OK, so you have made all these presuppositions. How do you know they are useful?

You will all know more about it when you stand up. That's right, on tiptoes. OK, sit down again.

Could someone analyse that series of presuppositions for us? Thank you, Sir John.

> "First, you presupposed that we wanted to know more about the usefulness of making presuppositions, and that we would all stand up, on tiptoes, to allow this to happen. Then you presupposed that we would all sit down again. Now we know that you were correct in presupposing that we would stand up and sit down, which checks those presuppositions. Which means we know that a presupposition is useful if we can check that it has taken effect, thus proving the first presupposition is right, and we do know more about it."

We are making presuppositions all the time. Sometimes they are obviously true – to us – from the context. Sometimes we are looking for confirmation. Vanessa, you have someone in your office for a job interview. What are you presupposing?

> "The person in front of me wants a specific job. I have advertised the vacancy in some way. The person has applied for

the job. Her qualifications and CV check out. It is worth my time interviewing this person."

What might the candidate be presupposing?

"That she knows all about the vacancy and the company. She wants the job. She is qualified for the job. She has a high enough chance of getting the job to make it worth coming to an interview."

Where do those presuppositions not necessarily match?

"In the details of the job – all the candidate knows so far is what was in the advertisement. That won't include the full terms, the job description or much idea of the working conditions and culture. I suppose it's also possible that there is a mistake – the person in front of me isn't who I think she is. I'd pick that up if I started feeling wrong about the situation."

There has to be some verbal checking, and we will also pick up on our cues that something is wrong. If we were consciously aware of them, we would probably note incongruities. There was the little gasp as you mentioned running a department of twenty people to someone who thinks the interview is for filing clerk. Remember the shake of the head when you addressed Roger as "Hello, John". Did you notice the clammy handshake of the dishwasher who is pretending to be a qualified chef?

Notice how *presuppositions* shade into *beliefs* and statements of *identity*. "I presuppose that I can count" goes to "I believe that I can do the accounts" and then to "I identify myself as an accountant". The *presuppositions* tend to need conscious checking: "Am I counting properly?" *Beliefs* are normally checked subconsciously and get questioned only by negation: "Am I doing the job if I am late producing the accounts?" *Identity* statements are rarely questioned – you *know* you are an accountant.

Exercise 3.5: Tracking Presuppositions

Here are a few ways that you can practise tracking presuppositions. Tape-record a few things that you say while you are working, dealing with the family and socialising, and sit down to analyse them for presuppositions. And spend some time listening to others – live, on radio or television, or on tape – and analyse their use of presuppositions. Then you can start to ask if you are matching others. How can you find out if you understand what they mean by their presuppositions? If you are getting them to match you, do they know what you are saying and how it affects them?

That will give you plenty to do until we meet again, to talk about matching states, feelings and values.

Day Four:
Valuing Their Emotions

Today we are going start to match *internal states* – such as values, feelings and emotions. Let's start with some definitions and a summary of what we are going to cover in this session.

• *Internal States*

Internal states include the way you feel – your emotions, values and criteria. These are different from the *internal processes* of arithmetic, logic and language that we considered last time. *State elicitation* is the way that we can recall and put on a state that we have experienced in the past. We will discuss appropriate states for *learning*.

• *Matching States*

Now we want to find out what state someone else is in. You will learn a useful condition for starting conversations, the *State of Curiosity and Wonder*. We can *calibrate* the other person's state from her physiology and by what she says, then attempt to *match* it internally by trying it on.

• *Anchoring*

Anchoring is the process by which we can change the mood we are in, using the *Circle of Excellence*, or help others to get into a better state. It involves recalling the appropriate state by means of an appropriate *trigger*.

• *Hierarchy of Values*

Some things are more important to you than others. You may value your family more highly than your work, or coffee more highly than tea. Some of these rankings may be inappropriate in particular contexts. You could put a high value on having a long lie-in on a Sunday: would it be appropriate if you should be on your way to work?

Before we start on the new material, I'd like to share some feedback from your experiences with outcomes. Paul, you have an experience to tell us about?

"Yes. You remember that I talked about my outcome of dressing more fashionably a couple of sessions ago. It made me feel better, and made it easier to contribute here. What I've realised is that my change in appearance and behaviour has been affecting the way other people deal with me. Some people are friendlier and others are more wary. I suppose they must feel differently about me. I hadn't realised that would happen when I set the outcome – I suppose there will always be consequences that we don't think of."

Thank you, Paul. Yes, we are never going to know all the results of our decisions, and we may have to adjust to our outcomes as we move towards them. We don't really know how we are going to feel about reaching the goal until it happens. Then we will be concentrating on a new outcome anyway. Life is a dynamic process.

Internal States

You know that logical thinking and gut feelings are different. People talk about being ruled by the heart or the head. So *internal state* differs from *internal process*. Last time, we found that internal process included thought, language and beliefs. This is the province of decisions, analysis and conscious processing. We can discuss them even though we may not know why we use particular sensing, linguistic or belief patterns. Internal state is less easy to find out about.

How do we represent internal states? First there are simple *feelings* – not the kinaesthetic sensations that we discussed in the last session, but the feelings of joy, sadness, anxiety, wonder and so on. Then there are the more complex feelings that we tend to call *emotions* – love, envy, sadness, and confidence. These are built up from a series of simple feelings. Finally, there are *values*. These tend to be statements, rather like beliefs in content, but with a strong emotional undertone that tells us that they must be true. These may be expressed as *morals* or *ethics*. Values, morals and ethics arise as an individual reacts to a situation (a *conscience* is evoked). People also have sets or systems of values which we might call *personality profiles*.

Exercise 4.1: Getting into a State

OK, while you're sitting there, be happy.

That wasn't all that easy, was it? Some of you weren't keen just to follow orders without being given a reason. Others tried to be happy but found that you didn't have a way to switch on your feelings. Some of you succeeded. No doubt each of you had a different method. Let me suggest one.

Most of us have had times in our life that we can look back on as happy. Some may have been happier times than others. They were states that we enjoyed, times when we were happier than we are now. So, just go back and remember a time when you felt really happy.

Most of you found that a great deal easier than just being told to be happy. The easiest way of getting into a state is to recall an appropriate experience from the past. That suggests a difficulty, though. What if we do not have a memory of a suitable experience? The first thing to do is to check whether we might have a different label for the state.

Go back to the experience you labelled as happy. Get right into that state. Now find a time when you were ecstatic. You can't find anything there? Just run through some synonyms in your mind. Try deliriously happy, excited and very happy, perfectly happy, or whatever else strikes you as being right.

Don't spend any longer in that state than you really want to!

The same memory may carry many labels, and we can add more labels to an existing memory if we want to. The experience will have been remembered in sensory specific terms. We are not immediately aware of all the details of the experience. In particular, we may be less conscious of the physiology and behaviours that we are exhibiting in the experience than, say, of what we saw. These physiological elements are important to the state. Once you can recall them, you can get fully into the state.

Let's do an exercise to help you to get into any mood that you want to take on.

Exercise 4.2: State Elicitation

Let's get some practice in *eliciting states* for each other – then you will know you can do it for yourself. Get together in pairs as Advisor and Client. You should remember that states are personal, so the easiest place to find them is in memory.

We'll start with the state of being happy. So the formula to use, with yourself or with others, is "Remember a time when you were happy", or "Remember a time when you felt happy". Give the Client time to find a suitable memory. You should see the physiology change when they have accessed it – look for a good smile.

The Advisor should get the Client to *associate* into the experience, get all the sensory–specific detail, and the thoughts and beliefs that go along with it. You can do that by moving the experience into the present: "Now you are feeling happy, what do you see, hear and sense round you? What do you think about this situation?" If what the person is saying gets too specific – the context is dominating the state – then get the subject to generalise by asking her to "Remember another time when you were happy." Pause and calibrate. "What is there about these memories that are similar?"

So, get the Client well associated into the happy state, then ask her to come back to the here and now. Change roles, and help the new Client into that state.

Amanada trying to "be happy"

OK, there is some feedback on that exercise. One or two of you were concerned about how long to leave the Client in the state. You can leave the Client plenty of time to appreciate pleasant states. If you need to get her to access difficult or painful states, try to get the information you need as quickly as possible. Then break the state by changing the subject completely. Ask her what she had for breakfast, tell her to jump up and down, get her to visualise a bunch of flowers or remember a joke. When you are eliciting a number of different states, finish with a pleasant and positive one.

We have discussed feelings, but what are emotions? In general terms, they are structures built from feelings, either happening together or in sequence. When we experience an event, or a memory, we often describe it in emotional terms.

Complexes of feelings include emotions, and states such as 'learning', which have multiple components. There are states about states, which Michael Hall calls *Meta-states*, such as feeling happy about being relaxed, being sad about feeling helpless, and feeling depressed about being depressed. Some of these are reinforcing, and some contradictory. Complex states also include *inclinations* and *moods*, which tend to be more permanent states, and *personality types*, which are even more fixed. In NLP, we often refer to positive states as *resources*. We can track the various representations of all these complexes, either by taking the emotion, mood or trait as a whole, or by breaking each one down into its component states.

Exercise 4.3: Learning State

Let's consider the state of learning. What is necessary for you in order to learn well? Go inside, and find a time when you were learning well. Now, ask yourself, what were the states that helped you to achieve that?

Call them out and I'll write them up on the board.

Confidence	**Relaxed**
Calm	**Happy**
Intelligent	**Competent**
Committed	**Moved**

Hopeful	In the mood
Bright	**Being helped**
Alert	Encouraged

OK, certainly most of those are states. Some are simple and some are complex in themselves. A couple of other things: 'bright' might be a sensory description, as well as a state. You might notice that some of these state names indicate a lead predicate system. Another of you came up with 'being helped'. This might be an indication of behaviour, a passive state, with the initiative coming from outside. It could also be a sense of drawing on internal resources.

Get back into your experience of being in a good learning state. Try adding in some of the resources that other people found useful for learning that you didn't come up with. Add them into the experience. Does that make it easier to learn?

Matching States

We have found out that we can improve our rapport, and so our communicating, by matching the physiology and the words that are used by the person we are talking to. It seems reasonable that the same is true of states – feelings, emotions and values.

In order to match a state, we need to have some way of recognising and calibrating the state in others, so that we don't just rely on the label. We have two sorts of information available - the physiology and behaviour of the Model, and the description that she gives us of the experience.

Here is a list of states to practise on:

Excitement	"Remember a time when you really felt excited."
Hunger	"Bring to mind a time when you felt really hungry."
Love	"Call up that moment when you knew you were in love."
Sadness	"Go back to a time when you were sad."

Excellence	**"Remember when you really excelled at something."**
Loss	**"Go back to an event where you felt a sense of loss."**
Hope	**"Bring to mind that time when you were especially hopeful."**

Exercise 4.4: Calibrating States

Work together in pairs as Advisor and Client.

For the first part of the exercise, the Client should take on one of the states listed above, without telling the Advisor which one. Get into the state and say the sentence "We had soup for dinner that day." The Advisor should guess which state the Client is in. Then repeat this for another four states. Then change over, so that the new Advisor has a chance to guess, from physiology and voice tone, five states that the new Client is in.

For the second part of the exercise, you will be trying to find out what the limits are to the state. The Advisor should ask the Client to take on a particular state. Then the Advisor will ask the Client to make small changes in expression, posture, breathing and voice tones. The Client should notice and report when the state changes and what it changes to. When you have experimented a few times, change roles and repeat for the new Client.

Most of you found that the state was quite limited in its physiological expression. You quickly lost it if you changed your posture, expression or breathing. If you behave differently, you feel different. If you want to change a bad state, perhaps all you have to do is move.

We know that each of us is experiencing one or more states all the time. The states that we are in will fit together into bigger chunks. They build up to emotions, moods, values and our whole personality. They are not necessarily all in harmony. We may experience internal conflicts, because the state we are currently in does not fit well into one of our higher-level chunks. If we are attending to someone else, while our value system says that we should be attending to ourselves, we may sense boredom or frustration – the internal equivalent of an incongruity signal.

If, in order to match someone else, we have to take on their set of states, there are likely to be conflicts with our personality. We will need to suspend the states that we generally have that would cause incongruity signals. One good way is to evoke a *State of Curiosity and Wonder*. In most people, this is sufficient to suspend the current states and allow new ones to be experienced.

> ### Exercise 4.5: State of Curiosity and Wonder
> Begin by doing some *self-pacing* (Exercise 1.2).
>
> Now, let yourself become curious about everything around you, and wonder how it all came about and how it all works. Be curious about what it is like to wonder, and wonder how you can be more curious. Then you can wonder what it is like to take on someone else's feeling states.
>
> Just consider the words that we use: we ask, "How do you feel?" or "How are you?" when we want information about someone's state. If we ask, "What do you feel?" or "What are you?" you will tend to get answers in the internal process field. If you think about it, *how* questions are at a higher level of complexity than *what* questions. They imply that a sequence, or structure of things, is present. The state 'happy' contains a number of physiological elements and behaviours, and it also includes thoughts and beliefs. And these components are personal – any two of us here will have different ways of thinking and acting 'happy'.

How then can we find out what someone else's state is, in order to match it? If they just tell us they are 'happy', what do we have to do to be in the same state?

Let's try guessing. That means bringing into awareness the state that *for us* most closely matches the words that the other person is using. First, calibrate the physiology. Does my posture, breathing, expression and behaviour match theirs? Am I comfortable using their voice tones: pitch, pace and volume? Then check the words, thoughts and beliefs. Am I comfortable using the sort of words that they are using? Could I take on their beliefs – just on a temporary basis, while we are talking? Can I share their values – again, in the moment?

The attitude to adopt is one of flexibility. You need to accommodate each new piece of evidence as it comes in. You are not trying to maintain a fixed state, but to go along with the state of the person you are communicating with.

It also doesn't really matter if the state is uncomfortable for you. You only need to maintain it until you are ready to lead the other person into a state where communicating will be easier.

OK, you are ready to take on your partner's state.

Exercise 4.6: Trying on a State

Work in pairs, as Model and Elicitor. The Model should choose a state in which she might be communicating. Do not name the state at this stage. Get into the state, and repeat the sentence "We had soup for dinner that day" a couple of times.

The Elicitor should calibrate the state. Become aware of the Model's expression, posture, breathing, movements and voice tone. Then the Elicitor should match the Model's physiology.

Next, the Model should talk about what it is like being in this state. Discuss the pictures, sounds and impressions that come to mind. Tell the Elicitor what you believe and know when you are in this state. The Elicitor should take on the representations and beliefs and be aware of the difference that these make to the state.

Then break the state, swap roles and repeat the exercise, with a different state, for the new Model and Elicitor.

So it does work, then? Did you notice the depth of rapport you can achieve by taking on the state, not just the physiology or the beliefs?

Just think how else you might get into a matching state, or set yourself up to deal with an important but unknown person. You have discovered that you have a whole range of useful states inside yourself, and we have learned how to find and install new ones. Now you are confronted with a real situation. How do you get access to the most useful state?

Anchoring

We can go back to considering outcomes. What is your outcome for the situation you are about to enter? What resources, what states, will make it easiest to achieve the outcome?

Let's take an example. Suppose you are going to make a public *presentation* – you will have to stand up in front of a dozen people to sell them something – a product, an idea, or something they should learn. What state would be useful for you? We'll write a list of them:

Calm	**Confident**
Happy	**Relaxed**
Raring to go	**Know everything I'm going to say to them**
Ready for anything	**Seeing my way ahead**
Lightness of spirit	**Determination**
Self-esteem	**Know my outcome**
They like me	**I want to listen and speak well**

OK, those are a great set of resources. All we have to do is to pick them up and take them with us into the meeting. First check – do you have access to all those resources? Think of a time when you were calm. OK. Go back to an experience of being happy. Good. And so on through the rest of the list. Where do you have gaps?

Right, so the problem areas are *confidence* and *self-esteem*. Several of you are saying that you can't remember being confident, or having self-esteem. Or is it that those feelings aren't strong enough? Let's start by finding out what it is you want to do confidently, and what self-esteem means to you.

Harry, what is it that you want to do confidently, and what is the nearest example that you can remember?

> "If I have to speak in public, I need to feel confident that I will get the words right, that I will make a good impression, and that I can answer any questions that come up. I haven't done much public speaking, and the times I have done it, I have been very nervous and put my foot in it. I have good experiences of talking to friends, and of one-to-one meetings with my manager."

So you have the resources, based on being confident with the words, the impression and the questions when there is only one other person there. Try getting into that experience, then put some other people into the background. Now let the person you are communicating confidently with drift into the background, and have one of the others come forward to talk to you. Is that OK? Good. In most meetings, you know whom you are speaking to at any point, and there will normally be only one person asking the question at any one time. Give yourself the resource of being confident with that significant person.

What is self-esteem? Paul, what do you mean by wanting more self-esteem?

> "I want to be able to see that I am not going to make a fool of myself. Every time I make a picture of myself in an important meeting, it looks bad. They are all staring at me, and I can't get the words out. I do see myself as confident in some meetings, where I am technically competent. Yes, when I can read the words in the script in my head."

So, you can remember meetings where you have prepared properly, and have presented the material with confidence. And when you have prepared what you are going to say, you can just read it off the screen in your head. When you have done that successfully, you have self-esteem. So you have appropriate experiences of self-esteem to use as a resource? That's very good.

Amanada, you also had a point about self-esteem.

"Yes. When I think of going into a business meeting, I see myself as being very small, and all the others in the room as being huge and overpowering. That makes me unable to speak properly when I get in there – everything comes out too fast and in a whisper. I have no problem speaking to people I see as being normal size."

Well, you are suggesting your own answer. Concentrate on the memories of times when the people in meetings were the right size and you gained self-esteem by being able to speak to them normally. Before you go into the meeting, just visualise the scene of being in a room with normal-sized people – that is what will happen anyway.

OK. You should all have a list of resource states and experiences that would be useful to take into the meeting. We are now going to *anchor* those, so you will always have them available to use. Anchoring is the process whereby we fix a link between a cue and a state: the state may be purely internal, or it may lead to a behaviour. The cue can be visual, auditory, kinaesthetic, olfactory, gustatory or digital. Let's see if we can find some that are common to all of us.

You are going along the road, and suddenly you see a red light in front of you. What happens? Yes, you stop – a brief warning state is triggered which tells your muscles to do something. They brake the car, or stop you walking off the curb. Then your brain catches up and makes sense of what has happened.

For an auditory cue, let's just remember Pavlov's dogs. They were conditioned to expect food when a bell rang, and so started salivating. Do you remember being at school when the lunch bell rang?

Now imagine you are in the kitchen. You reach out to pick up the kettle. But instead of being cold, the metal is hot – someone else has just made a cup of tea. You go into a state of pain, and drop the kettle, so that you don't burn yourself any more.

Back to food again. As you go along the High Street, you begin to smell newly baked bread, and feel hungry. Or you get the aroma of freshly ground coffee and feel thirsty. Or perhaps your stomach revolts at one or the other.

Now just imagine you are floating in the sea. And suddenly your mouth is full and salty. The state could be panic – you might believe you were drowning, and you would try to get your head above water. All those state and behavioural reactions are linked directly to sensory input, with thoughts and beliefs coming into consciousness later. Digital input can have the same effect.

"FIRE!"   **"JACKPOT!"**   **"REDUNDANCY"**

I'll bet that each of those words changed your state to some extent.

These anchors have all been set by experience, as a result of a single powerful event or by repetition. This suggests that if we want to set anchors deliberately, we can use the same process.

We have already seen that any of the **[VAKOGD]** channels can be used to trigger the anchor. Very often, the trigger is in more than one sensory system, for reinforcement, and in case we miss one of the signals. A green traffic light will often be reinforced by a sound – a bleep for pedestrian lights, or a horn blowing behind you when you are driving. You don't just smell the bread – you might see a loaf in the shop window, or read a sign saying "BREAD". If you are drowning, you will get a series of kinaesthetic signals as well as a salt taste. So, if you want to set up a strong anchor, you might want to use several triggers.

What might you want to use as a trigger for the states for a meeting? First think about where you want the states to kick in: at your desk, on your way to the meeting, going through the door into the room, or when you are actually in position in the meeting. Think what external triggers there might be in the place where you want to fire the anchor. What will you see, what noises will you hear, what kinaesthetic signals will be available? Don't forget, if you use something common as a trigger, you will get into the state frequently. This could happen if you set the trigger to be seeing a door, hearing a door close, or sitting in a chair. This may or may not be useful.

On the other hand, if you set something very specific as the trigger, such as seeing a particular painting, hearing someone's voice or touching a unique doorknob, what will happen if that person or object is not there? This is another reason for using a compound trigger, comprising a common visual, auditory or kinaesthetic cue plus one or more key words. I would tend to use seeing an audience, hearing the meeting start, or a touch on a particular knuckle, plus the word indicating the particular state, as my 'stage anchors'.

There are a number of ways of setting anchors – you can probably devise your own strategies, as long as you bear in mind that you are aiming to experience the required state, and the required trigger, simultaneously.

Exercise 4.7: Circle of Excellence

This is a solo exercise – I'll give you the instructions as we go along. Get into the posture that you will be in when you trigger the anchor – probably sitting or standing. Make sure there's a clear patch of floor in front of you.

In this position, decide what the triggers are going to be. Visualise the picture; imagine the sounds or feelings. If you are going to set a touch anchor on your own body, work out where that is going to be and what it will feel like. Decide on the key words. I recommend that you use triggers in at least two different modalities.

Now imagine a circle in front of you, into which you can put all the resources you are going to need in the meeting. Elicit the first state you want to use. Concentrate until you are really there in the state, and put it into the circle. Now go back and find another example of that state. It is so useful to you. When you are really in there, put that into the circle. Yes, you can have another example – go back, get into it, put it in the circle.

Remember a time when you had your next resource. You are in a very resourceful time. As you are at the peak of the experience, you can preserve that for the future by placing it in the circle. Now recall another similar example – perhaps an even better one... And you can keep putting these into the Circle of Excellence until you have all the resources that you need.

Set the triggers, and move the Circle of Excellence until it is inside you, and you have taken it into every cell of your body.

OK, you've enjoyed that quite long enough. Break the state. Jump up and down. Now sit down and imagine you are having tea with the Queen.

Right, so you have a meeting coming up: you are going to tell the group everything that you have learned about communicating. Fire your anchors. Imagine coming up to the front of the room and speaking for 10 minutes. Now go back to your seats.

That was a lot easier than you thought it would be, wasn't it? Didn't that make it a lot easier to consider all the ways that you might match the people in your next meeting? And so you now know how to prepare for that sort of thing in the future, don't you?

These possibilities all lead to ideas for practice outside this session. Try passively calibrating others' states. You can take note of the state of people you are with, from the cues that they give, without having to ask them any questions. Then you can practise getting into those states either at the time, or later in private.

At home, you could model a TV actor or personality while they are appearing on the screen. You might want to work with your partner, a colleague or a friend to run through the formal elicitation exercises. As always, practise until you can match someone else's state without having to be consciously aware of how you are doing it.

For homework on the Circle of Excellence, choose at least one other context where you would like to have a better state than usual, select the anchors and resources and install them.

Hierarchy of Values

It may be useful to find out what is most important to someone in a particular context. We could match his values, especially by making sure that what we are saying is positive and important to him. We might even need to change his values, or at least change their order of importance, to achieve our outcome.

Exercise 4.8: Work Values
Ask yourself, "What do I value about the way I work? What is really important to me?" Take a piece of paper and write down what is important to you about the way you work. List your ideas in a column, and leave room to add comments.

Have you all got some? Good. Just shout some out and I'll write them up here:

Freedom to do it my way	**A close group**
Making good money	**A good structure**
Good teamwork	**Beating the competition**
Happy in my work	**Just glad to have a job**
Making use of my skills	**Doing a good job**
Helping the company	**Getting good feedback**
Helping myself	**Being a breadwinner**

OK. There's a good mixture of things there. You have noted some *behaviours* – making money, using skills. There are also some *beliefs* – freedom to do it my way, helping the company. Quite a few of you have *feeling* words – freedom, close, good, happy. So values can be described in terms of each of the systems that we are considering – behaviours, thoughts and states. And notice something else. The words that you are using are mostly non-specific. They cannot be sensed directly, but are abstractions and generalisations. *You* know what you mean by good money and skills: I can only *guess* what you mean, based on my own experience.

Values systems are quite personal, but there have been many attempts to systematise them over the last few decades. Generally the components include:

Attention – Inwards to self or outwards to others, things or ideas
Choice – On the basis of activities, thoughts or feelings
Action – Proactive, towards a good state, or reactive, away from a bad state

Prudence, would you like to tell us all about what is important to you about the way you work. We will all listen out for the way

Prudence is attending, where her concerns are, how she makes choices and takes action.

> "Well, I like the people I work with: we are a close-knit team. They can tell me where I'm doing a good job. I feel the company is doing something important for its customers, and that I am contributing to that. I like to feel comfortable with what I'm doing, and make others feel comfortable as well."

Thank you. Her *attention* seems to be largely outwards to others – the team, the customers. Just as a check, Prudence, what do you do when you want to relax? You go out with some friends. An internally attending person would probably do something alone. The important *choices* seem to be made on the basis of feelings and values. The words she used for *action* were positive – like, good, important, and comfortable – things she is moving towards.

PS, could you please read out your list of what is important to you about the way that you work.

> "Making good money. Satisfying my customers. Beating the opposition. Freedom of action."

There are a number of different things there – some inwards directed and some outwards. Focus on self, others and money. Some choices based on thought, and some on feelings. We can find out what PS emphasises by establishing his *Hierarchy of Values*. The questioning goes like this:

PS, if you had to choose between something that *made you good money* but didn't *satisfy your customers*, and something else which satisfied your customers but didn't make you good money, which would you choose?

> *"Money."*

If you had to choose between something that *beat the opposition* but didn't give you *freedom of action*, and something that gave you freedom of action but didn't beat the opposition, which would you choose?

"More difficult, but *freedom*."

If you had to choose between something that *made you good money* but didn't give you *freedom of action*, and something that gave you freedom of action but didn't make you good money, which would you choose?

"*Money*."

You can begin to see a pattern, with "Making good money" being the most important value. We can go on, contrasting each possible pair of values and counting the number of times each is chosen, until we have worked out the whole list. I would guess that his full hierarchy is: 1. Making good money. 2. Having freedom of action. 3. Beating the opposition. 4. Satisfying my customers. That doesn't mean that satisfying his customers is unimportant, just that other things are more important.

Why don't you try putting your work values into a hierarchy? Just a word of warning, if you have more than about five, contrasting all the possible pairs can get a bit tedious, so start by dividing the values into 'more important' and 'less important'. Rank them within those two groups first, then check where the overlap comes.

Exercise 4.9: Ranking Values
Get together in pairs, an Expert and a Questioner. The Expert should give the Questioner the notes from Exercise 4.8.

The Questioner will take any two values 'A' and 'B', and ask, "If you had to choose between something that 'A' but didn't give you 'B', and something that gave you 'B', but didn't 'A', which would you choose?" Put a tick beside the value preferred by the Expert. Then ask the same question for each pair of values. For four values, you will ask six questions; for five values, ten questions. Then rank the values by the number of ticks that they received.

Once you have done that, change round and elicit the hierarchy of values for the second Expert. Take about 20 minutes in total.

Were there any difficulties? Good. Were there any surprises? A few of you didn't realise what was really important until you were offered stark choices. I wonder what will happen when you work out the hierarchy of values for your family and social activities, and for your life as a whole?

So, people have feelings, emotions, moods, personality traits and values that we can elicit. We know that the better we match them, the better we will communicate with them. So now we need to find out how we can elicit, evoke and match internal states.

Next time, we will start to look at pacing, and gathering information that you will use to achieve your optimal strategies for communicating. We will be concentrating on physiology and external behaviour, and learning about processes, strategies and logical levels.

Day Five:
Patterns of Behaviour

For this session, and the next two, we are going to concentrate on pacing – working to understand other people. We need to know how they behave, what they know and believe, and how they feel. You will build on what you have already discovered, and maybe find some new or improved ways to communicate. Remember, though, that they are people, with their own ways of doing things, and their own beliefs and feelings. You should be sensitive to their reactions. If you start getting signs of unease, anger or inattention, go back to pacing their physiology, agree with their content and language and match their mood. Then find a new way of getting the information that you want.

This time, we will be concentrating on non-verbal information, and the non-verbal processing of sensory information. We will be finding out how people do things, and analysing their skills. The main items we will be covering are:

• *Pacing Behaviour*

Pacing is a learning process. When we pace what people do, we may learn skills from them or find out how they react to various situations. One of the best tools we have for discovering how people do things is *eye-accessing cues*.

• *Skills*

Skills are a sequence of behaviours and internal representations that enable us to carry out a task effectively. You are probably unaware of some of your own skills. We will learn about tracking the details of strategies, particularly *decision strategies*, the sequences that allow us to make choices and come to conclusions.

• *Habits*

Habits are another sequence of behaviours and representations. We are normally completely unaware of the details of a habit. Drawing out the reasons behind them allows us to control, change or even install new habits. You will learn a technique called *Satisfying Your Purpose* to help you to change habits.

We started the course with the assumption that the mind and body are one system. The body, in this case, includes the physical structure of our brain, together with our muscular and nervous system, and the effect that our body can have on its environment by existing, moving and speaking. The mind includes all our sensing, thinking and feeling. We have already found out how much we can tell about someone else's internal – mind – processes, by looking, listening and sensing externally what their body is doing.

I know some of the techniques you have learned still seem difficult to use in practice. This is natural, while you are in the period of learning. You have skills, from your business and social life as well as the ones you are learning here, and today's session will be mainly about eliciting, analysing and teaching strategies and skills. Just take a moment to think about the skills you have – in making decisions and carrying out physical tasks.

Pacing Behaviour

You can pace behaviour by finding out the details of the activity and what lies behind it. Does anyone have an example of a behaviour you don't understand? Yes, Stephen?

> "One of our contractors keeps being late with deliveries and holding up production. My outcome was to see him and find out what the problem is. Well, I had a face-to-face chat, and told him we are looking for better punctuality. I thought I'd made myself clear, but there was no improvement in the delivery times. I saw him again, after our last session, and thought that I'd appeal to his values. He showed me that he cared a lot about the quality of his production, but I noticed, from his language, that time is a low priority in his values system. He used clichés like 'More haste, less speed' and 'You can't rush a good job'. I tried to explain our priorities, but I'm not sure it made any difference. How should I have put it to him?"

You can alter the hierarchy of values, either for yourself or others, and we'll look at that in a later session. For the moment, just consider what his highest value is. It might be fear of losing the contract, or the benefits of getting the money from Whizzitts. If you can tie delivery time to that top value, you will motivate him to do it. Whether you use a threat or a bribe, make sure you see that it is firmly linked to delivery times *in his mind* before you end the meeting. Then, don't forget to measure the performance to make sure that his behaviour has changed.

So far, we have concentrated on physiological matching of what someone is doing, with the idea of building rapport. We can calibrate for more detail if we need to. Look for changes in skin colour, in posture, in the face, and in breathing rates or position.

In order to pace behaviour and skills, we need to learn how to read physiological cues and elicit information about what is going on when somebody is doing something. We then have to put the information together into structures used by the subject and useful to us, so that we can build a model of what is happening.

The first sources of information we are going to look at are called *eye-accessing cues*. There seems to be a regular pattern of eye movements that indicate the sensory system that people are using, and these tie up with other physical patterns.

Exercise 5.1: Eye-Accessing Cues

We are going to work in threes, and establish what these *eye-accessing cues* are for ourselves and our partners. Take it in turns to be the Questioner, the Model and the Observer.

The first Questioner should take Handout 5.1, and ask each of the questions in Section One in turn. The Model does not need to answer out loud, so long as she knows what the answer is. It is the job of the Observer to note the movement of the Model's eyes while the question is being asked and until an answer is forthcoming. Get in a position where you can see clearly, and ask the Model to keep her eyes open during the process.

continued...

Worksheet 5.1:   *Eye Movements*

Model:

Questions	Eye Movements

Section One
1. What colour was your first front door?
2. What was shown in the last TV advert that you saw?   _____
3. Can you describe what sound an owl makes?   _____
4. Hum your favourite love song.   _____
5. Feel the first snow of winter.   _____
6. How does hot bread taste?   _____
7. Tell yourself to stand up straighter.   _____
8. What do you say to yourself when you are early?   _____
9. Hear a clatter, two bongs and a woof.   _____
10. Imagine your favourite love song played at double speed.   _____
11. What colour is grapefruit and gooseberry cordial?   _____
12. Picture a cross-Channel roller coaster.   _____

Section Two
1. What colour was your family's first car?   _____
2. Can you describe one of the adverts in this morning's paper?_____
3. What did your best friend at school sound like?   _____
4. Sing the music of the national anthem.   _____
5. What is it like having a hot shower?   _____
6. Describe the effect of having a cold fizzy drink.   _____
7. Tell yourself that tomorrow is another day   _____
9. What would a ring, two beeps and a bellow sound like?   _____
10. Imagine hearing your mother with gruff, bass voice.   _____
11. What would you see if the Albert Hall were a coconut?   _____
12. See yourself painting vertical red stripes on that wall.   _____

Section Three
1. What is the first poster that you remember seeing?   _____
2. Can you describe the colour of your bedroom door?   _____
3. What did your last boss sound like?   _____
4. Whistle your favourite TV theme tune.   _____
5. Feel the pebbles of a beach between your toes.   _____
6. What is it like to eat ice cream?   _____
7. Tell yourself that learning is fun.   _____
8. What do you say to yourself when you feeling happy?   _____
9. Can you hear two quacks, a snort and a bleat?   _____
10. What would your favourite record sound like at half speed?   _____
11. Visualise a paddle steamer on a yellow sea.   _____
12. What would a five-legged zebra look like?   _____

Diagram 5.1: Eye-Accessing Patterns

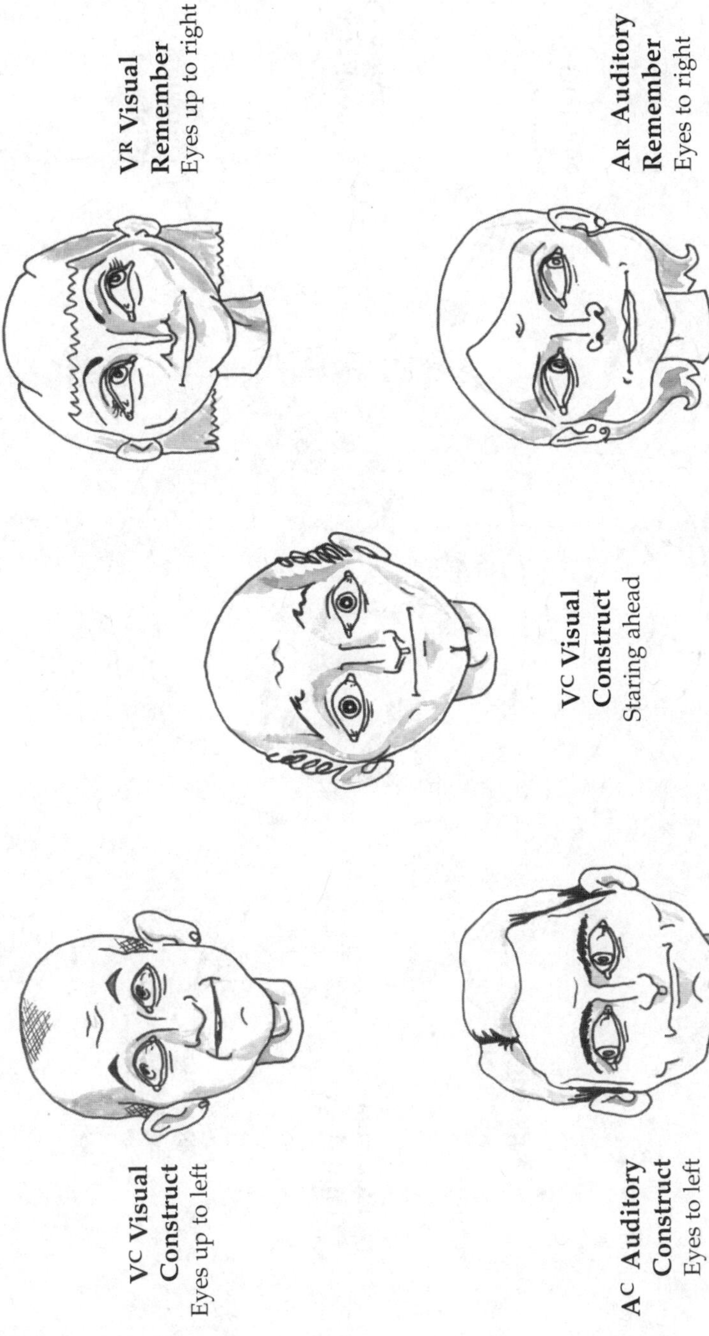

V^R Visual Remember Eyes up to right

A^R Auditory Remember Eyes to right

V^C Visual Construct Staring ahead

V^C Visual Construct Eyes up to left

A^C Auditory Construct Eyes to left

Diagram 5.2 Eye Movements

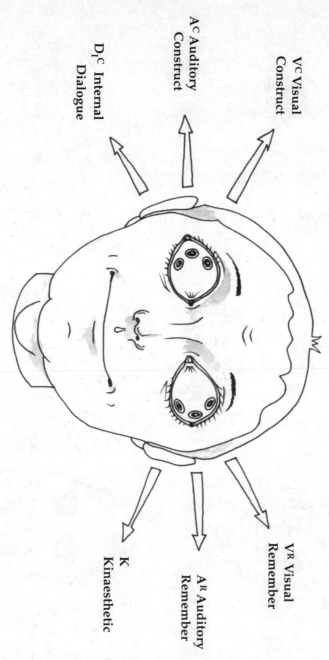

V^C Visual
Construct

A^C Auditory
Construct

D$_I$^{C} Internal
Dialogue

V^R Visual
Remember

A^R Auditory
Remember

K
Kinaesthetic

Exercise 5.1 *continued...*

The eyes may move left or right, they may also roll up or down. They may widen into a stare. Diagram 5.1 shows the principal possibilities. The Observer should use words or arrows beside each question on the Worksheet to indicate what has happened. Once the Observer has noted the movements, the Questioner should move on to the next question.

When the Model has been asked all the questions in Section One, change roles. The Model becomes the Questioner, the Questioner becomes the Observer, and the Observer the new Model. The new Questioner should then ask the questions in Section Two of the worksheet, and the Observer should make notes.

Once you have finished the questions in Section Two, change roles again, so that the final Questioner asks questions to the new Model from Section Three of the worksheet. Then give the marked worksheets to the Models.

So, what did you see? Some quite complicated movements. Probably not too much like Diagram 5.1. Let's go through that and find out what theory says. The first two questions asked about *visual memory*. The diagram shows this as looking up to your right (to the left of the person having the memory, but all these drawings have been made from the viewpoint of the observer). The next two asked about *remembered sound*. This is shown as looking level to the right. Then you were asked to have an *internal dialogue*. Most people will do this looking down to the right. Questions 7 and 8 were about what you are feeling *kinaesthetically*. This usually involves looking down to the left. Next came two invitations to invent something you could hear. Like a remembered sound, the *auditory constructed* response is level, but looking to the left. Finally, you were asked to make two *constructed visual* images. These are usually made looking upwards to the left, although some people will do it staring straight forward, with their eyes defocused.

What did you actually see? Probably some rapid eye movements as the subject considered the question, and used their lead system to find the information. Just before the subject started to answer, you should have seen their eyes move to the appropriate position.

If you found most of the responses were reversed from left to right, so that the subject was generally looking to the left for the first six replies and to the right for the second six, and the subject is naturally left-handed, they are what is called *reverse-wired*. Because of this phenomenon of reverse wiring, it is worth checking the responses of anyone that you want to calibrate in this way. The most reliable questions to distinguish reverse wiring are kinaesthetic and internal dialogue ones: sometimes people have to construct something that you think they will remember, or go into memory for pieces of the image that you have asked them to invent. You have a question, Amanada?

> "My partner seemed to be showing movements that I wasn't expecting to see. There didn't seem to be any consistency in his visual accessing, and even for internal dialogue and kinaesthetic responses, he sometimes seemed to be swapped over."

OK. Don't forget that you are only guessing what processing will happen when you ask the questions: you are then calibrating to find out what did happen. Suppose you asked him to remember a picture. He might have searched for it and not been able to find it. Then he could have spoken to himself about the memory, suddenly felt what triggered it, looked in his memory again, failed to see it, and finally constructed something to answer your question. So you were expecting a visual remembered response, with the eyes up to the right. His actual eye movements were something like up right, down left, down right, up right, up left. Or asking for a kinaesthetic memory of sand and actually getting a dialogue: "What is sand like? Oh, yes, it's warm and gritty". His eyes move down left, not down right. You are making presuppositions when you look for eye-accessing cues. Like all presuppositions, they need to be checked.

It takes quite a lot of practice to use eye-accessing cues automatically to give you good information. When you have learned to do it, you will begin to get a lot of information about the way people think. Start by remembering Diagram 5.2, which summarises the processing for someone who is normally wired.

What else did you notice? You might have seen that the eye movements are matched by other changes in the body. When someone is accessing visually, their body and head tend to move up and back, with the hands also held higher. Speaking tends to speed up and be higher in pitch. By contrast, someone who is processing kinaesthetic data, or talking to themselves, will tend to be hunched, with the head lowered and hands down. The voice becomes deeper and slower. The position for auditory accessing is more neutral, but you might notice his hands in a position where they might hold a telephone.

So, how will these eye-accessing cues help you to pace the person you are talking to?

First, you are connecting what they say to the system they are processing in. If you switch to that predicate system, it may help you to understand some of the references. It will also improve the way that you match that person. Second, you are beginning to learn how they process in a particular context: if they are doing something that you want to model, you will have to learn to do it their way.

The following is an exercise that you can do at any time when you can reasonably look closely at someone who is talking, without embarrassing either party. While you practise you will be looking for how the person processes information, not listening to what they are telling you. Try calibrating a celebrity or a politician on television.

Exercise 5.2: Looking for Information

Get together in pairs, Model and Calibrator. If you weren't working together in the last exercise, start by calibrating each other's eye-accessing cues.

Then the Model simply has to talk for five minutes on any topic that interests them. The Calibrator has two tasks. First, set yourself to monitor the verbal predicates that the Model is using. At the same time, look for the eye-accessing cues. See if they match the verbal predicates, or whether there are any incongruities. After five minutes, you can briefly discuss the incongruities. Then change roles, and repeat the exercise for the new Calibrator.

Skills

Two sets of behaviour that we may be interested in pacing are skills and habits. Skills are sets of behaviour that carry out a particular task effectively. Habits are sets of behaviour that are carried out largely unconsciously, and may or may not be currently useful to the person doing them. Reading, driving and smoking include a number of behaviours that are done habitually. Skills and habits are each composed of a number of steps, whether we are aware of them or not. These steps may be purely cognitive, purely behavioural or both. Normally, there will be a sign that can be calibrated, even if the step is a cognitive one such as looking for an internal picture: this will give an eye-accessing cue.

One very common skill is the *decision strategy*. We all make frequent decisions. Most of them we make without being aware of it at all. A decision strategy is a sequence of operations. It always starts with a *trigger*. This is something that makes you aware that you have to take a decision. The trigger could be external, such as the waiter asking you what you want to order, or seeing that your shoes are wearing out. It could also be internal, like imagining lying on a sunny beach or feeling hungry. Then there is a period of *operation*. This allows you to become aware of the possible choices. Again, it could be internal or external. You may have to go and collect information, or it may all be in your memory. Then there is a *test*. You take each alternative and use some sort of comparison process to accept or reject it. There may be several rounds of operation and testing. Then you *exit* the process. The decision has been made and you move on to implement it.

In order to analyse a decision strategy, we must know what steps there are in it, beginning with the trigger, including the operational and test steps, and ending with the way that we exit it.

Exercise 5.3: Buying Strategy

Get into pairs, one as Model and the other as Observer. The Model is going to imagine that they are about to buy something – perhaps a new car. You have a genuine choice to make between makes and models, and you have the skill to make a good decision.

Both should start by writing down on separate pieces of paper the context in which the decision is being made . The Observer should take mental notes of what you calibrate as physiological cues. The Model should take mental notes of the steps of the decision. Once the decision strategy is completed, both write out these mental notes in the order of the steps.

As Model, you should silently rehearse each stage you go through in deciding which one you are going to buy. Indicate to the Observer when you start and finish the decision-making process.

Once you have both finished writing notes, compare the two lists. Try to fit the internal process to the external signs. Go through the decision strategy again, with the Model talking through the steps, and the Observer pointing out where there is evidence of eye-accessing or other cues, with no step being reported. Go on until you agree that you have noted all the steps from trigger to exit.

Then change roles and repeat the exercise for the new Model's decision strategy.

OK, so what did you see? In a way, this exercise would have been easier to do on your own with a mirror. Then you could match up what you were thinking about doing with the changes you could see in your face and body. One important thing to note from this exercise is the *signal* that tells you that your decision is *correct*. It could be visual, auditory or kinaesthetic. Make sure you can distinguish it from signals that tell you that you are on the way to a right answer, or that this option is the best of a bad job.

Would someone like to give us a run-through of his decision strategy? John, what was your process?

"Mine was quite simple. I was choosing a new car. I saw remembered pictures of cars, and heard a voice saying 'uh-huh' or 'no'. That gave me a short list of four models. Then I saw myself driving each one, and felt what it would be like to be in it. Again, the voice gave me a yes or no. Then the car I wanted flashed into my mind in full details and the right colour. How did I know it was the right one? Everything about it was right. What was the final internal signal? A loud 'YES', and some music, from behind my head. Did I really say that? I wasn't aware of that until now."

That's an excellent description. A personal strategy, and an effective one by the sound of it. And enough detail so that we can all try it out, or model it on ourselves. Why don't we try it together? We can generalise it to fit any of the things we were making decisions about.

Start by remembering the pictures of various things you have seen that you might want to buy. As each picture comes to mind, let an internal voice tell you whether to put it on a shortlist.

OK, now you have a short list, bring the pictures to mind again, but this time associate. See what you see when you are with or inside your potential purchase; hear the noises and voices, feel the sensations, listen for that internal voice that will make the decision. And when it has made the decision, it will give you a picture of exactly what your purchase should be, and tell you, with a fanfare, that this is for you.

Right, how many of you did that work for? Yes, mainly people who prefer to work with visual images. The people whose representations are more kinaesthetic probably didn't feel quite right when they tried on John's strategy. But at least by taking it on, you could pace what was happening for John while he made the decision.

So why would we want to know how John is making decisions? Several possibilities spring to mind. John might be very successful at his job, which involves taking decisions. If we know how he takes decisions, perhaps we can learn that strategy for ourselves, or learn to teach it to other people. Perhaps someone we work with is confident about taking decisions, but is generally wrong about the outcome. We might want to work through their strategy and find out what needs to be changed in order for them to choose better. Or perhaps we are trying to manage someone who is very bad at taking decisions at all. Maybe it would help to find out how they are doing it, so we can help them to add another way of choosing.

Habits

There are two reasons why we might want to calibrate someone else's habit. First, we might want to match it in some way, so as to deepen our rapport. We have already learned that matching simple repetitive behaviours such as finger tapping can get us much closer. Second, we might want to lead him away from the habit. To do that, we will have to find what benefits he gets from the habit are useful to him and find other ways of achieving them.

Has someone got an example of a habit in a work context that needs changing? Ruth, you have something that you would like to share with us?

"Yes, it's about my boss – who isn't on this course! He has a habit of coming and standing next to my desk when I am busy. He just looks out of the window and whistles tunelessly. Then, after a few minutes, he goes back into his office. When I ask him if wants anything, he just says 'No' and goes away. My outcome is to have a strategy that gets him to come out and talk to me when he has something to say."

107

OK, this seems to be a case for leading rather than matching. No doubt he would react in some way if you matched him either by standing at your desk, or his desk, peering out of the window and whistling. The question is, do you want to find out what the reaction would be?

Consider what his state is when he comes out. Is he bored? If so, would he just wander off when you spoke to him? It sounds more as if he is deeply involved in resolving something inside – absorbing information or making decisions. You would need to find out what part the habit played in this. This is simple mind-reading, but he might have to put internal pictures of the alternatives against a particular piece of scenery that is only visible from your window, and hold himself in a particular state by whistling. With the skills you are learning on this course, you could help him to reset his anchors to things that annoy you less.

We'll finish off this session by trying a technique that helps you to generate new or better ways of doing things and still satisfy your purpose in doing them. As you remember, we only have a real choice when there are at least three ways of moving forward. You could use one of these ways to change habits or other behaviours that you would like to improve. Make sure that you are aware of your correct decision signal (from Exercise 5.3).

Exercise 5.4: Satisfying Your Purpose

You can do this on your own. Choose a habit or behaviour that you want to change. Ask yourself, "Would I change this behaviour if I had something better to put in its place?" Make sure you get a positive signal.

Then go inside and ask your unconscious mind, "What is the positive purpose of the behaviour?" Once you have an answer, ask it to come up with at least three other ways of behaving to achieve the same purpose. Then preview each of the new ways of behaving. Associate in, and find out what it is really like to behave this way. Consider the consequences for yourself and for other people. Go on generating alternatives until you have at least three that give you a positive signal.

If you cannot get positive signals, it may be that the existing behaviour has another purpose, so go inside and discover that, then generate some more ways of achieving that purpose.

Once you have enough new ways of behaving, choose the best for you. Now ask yourself, "When will I make the change?" The answer may come in words, pictures or feelings. It may give you a time, or some event that has to happen first.

Take notes of the behaviour that will replace the habit you dislike, and the time that you are going to make the change. When the time comes, make sure the change is for the better.

The constant theme of this course is that the more you practise, the more automatic these tools will be in use. Now you have the skills to go out and find better ways to practise, and in learning from others you will learn better how to do it for yourself – and enjoy that learning and doing.

Now is the time to review all the outcomes that you have set yourself in the first half of the course, and find out how you can achieve them. So have a wonderful experience of discovery, and come back next time to learn all about pacing language.

Day Six:
Structures of Language

Some of you are beginning to see why we are learning these techniques, as you hear your communicating improving. Others may find that you are getting on better with important people. You may become aware that your work is improving, and that you feel better in yourself about what you are saying.

Today we are going to look at language, and use questioning techniques to fill in the gaps in what we are being told about people's strategies, thoughts, beliefs and presuppositions. This will help us to understand the person we are speaking to, and help that person to know what they want from us. This is what we are going to cover:

• *Deletion, Generalisation and Distortion*

The brain seems to store both raw sensations (pictures, sounds, smells, etc.) and digital information (numbers and words). It doesn't seem to store everything that we have witnessed, and obviously it can't store things that we haven't witnessed. There are layers of translation between the experience and the language that we use to report the experience. This translation changes the experience: information is *deleted* (not stored or not reported), *generalised* (experiences are added together to form a composite) and *distorted* (usually by drawing false conclusions from evidence). The whole process is called *filtering*. We will experience some of these filters in action with *Chinese Whispers* and *Mimes*.

• *Language Models*

Language models are tools for finding information that is lost by filtering. They provide a series of questions to fill in the gaps that people leave when they speak. You will use John McWhirter's *Basic Fractal Language Model*. You can use these questions to get extra information – the purpose of *pacing*. We might also want to show that our partners in conversation are misunderstanding something that is important to us. You will see how deletion, generalisation and distortion are used deliberately in advertising, and see how the message is changed when we ask the right questions. You will then practise the techniques for *coaching*.

• *Beliefs*

Beliefs can range from the everyday presuppositions in our language (e.g. that we know what is meant by "my car") to the certainties by which we live (I know that the sun will rise tomorrow morning). You will learn to listen for beliefs, and the language patterns that imply beliefs. These include *equations* (parts of the verb 'to be'), *modal operators* (such as 'must' and 'should'), *universal quantifiers* (such as 'always', 'none' and 'every'), *comparatives* and *superlatives*. There are also the *connections* patterns of the Basic Fractal Language Model.

Deletion, Generalisation and Distortion

Language is the way we store, and can manipulate, digital information. Input is from our sensations, internally translated, and from the digital output of others, spoken or written. It is filtered through our mind, by physical limitations on what we can process, by our existing knowledge, and by our own preferences.

The amount of digital data in the world is very large. There are nearly five billion people out there. Most people speak at well over a hundred words per minute. Even if we only speak for two hours a day, that means we have an output of at least four million words a year. That is equivalent to each of us producing at least forty books full of information. To keep up with everything said or written, we would have to process two hundred billion books full of information every year. We can't cope with that scale of input. So we must limit what to expose ourselves to.

Some of this filtering happens by chance. We can only witness conversations with people that are within earshot, either present or by telephone or broadcast. We can only read words that are visible to us – we have to have access to the book, computer or television screen, magazine or advertising hoarding. Without technology, we cannot get information from people four offices, three houses or a continent away. Without a common language, we have great difficulty making sense of any input, and we would probably consciously filter out most of it.

Some of the filtering is by choice – we have some control over whom we are physically near and whom we telephone. In a party, we choose which conversation to listen to: at home we have control over which radio or television channel we listen to or watch, which book, magazine or Website we read. We may choose because of need – it might be part of our job – or for pleasure. Some people prefer to watch television dramas rather than read computer manuals written in Flemish.

But just because we are exposed to all this information, that doesn't mean that we remember it or could reproduce it all again. The hard disk on my desktop computer can store 3.5 gigabytes of information, about half a billion words – thank goodness I don't have to read them all. My brain certainly can't store everything, although libraries and computers can make it available to me if I know what I need.

In practice, the information that we are exposed to is processed as it is heard or seen. Much of what we hear or read is forgotten immediately – *deleted* from our consciousness. What we do hear is *generalised* – being changed according to context or put together from several different sources – or *distorted* by our internal processing before being stored.

In the same way, what we say or write is governed by the way that we process language. We do not notice all the deletions, generalisations and distortions that we make as we tell other people about what we know and about ourselves. When we hear someone else, though, we notice some of their processing because their pattern of deletions, generalisations and distortions is different from ours.

Exercise 6.1: Chinese Whispers

Form a large circle, and we'll play *Chinese Whispers*. I'll start by whispering a message to Apricot. She will repeat it to Amanada and so on round the circle. Just so we can't overhear each other, I'd like everyone except the person who is speaking the message to keep reciting the alphabet backwards as quietly as they can.

OK, the original message was "NLP is the science of excellence in communicating, so we should all be excellent at passing this message round the circle". The message that reached Sir John was

"The May King signs a common version going round". Harry, you are about the halfway mark – what was it when you heard it?

"Sorry, I don't really remember – something about making the size of communiqués?"

So, interference from our own thoughts, and the passage of time shorten the message by deleting parts of it; the meaning becomes distorted as we try to make sense of it; and we may only be left with a generalised impression of what was said to us.

So what information do we get? It is either direct sensations or digital data that we receive verbally or in writing. This is only a small subset of all possible data. We will only input those things that we are exposed to, and are concentrating on. We will not store a picture of the landscape in front of us if we have our eyes shut, or are looking at a book. There will be no memory of a sound if we were asleep or singing to ourselves when it was made. This kind of deletion cannot be recovered from memory, however hard we try, because the data was never input in the first place.

What we may do is construct a false memory of the event, based on other similar instances, what we subsequently are told or read and preferences of our own. We can only tell that something is being constructed if we are conscious of the process as we do it, and label it as a construction: after that, it is simply a memory, with a visual remembered eye-accessing cue.

The data that we do have available for input are filtered on the way to memory. Parts of the information may seem irrelevant or duplicated and are deleted. Our processing preferences will dictate whether we emphasise visual, auditory, kinaesthetic or digital inputs. Deleting the detail from the less preferred systems does the emphasising. For digital data, things that we do not understand may be deleted – information stated in less-favoured predicate systems, vocabulary that we do not normally use, things that we are not interested in. States – that is, combinations of sensory and digital data – may be disregarded if they are too alien. Situations of acute physical and mental pain may be ignored, leaving a blank. The memory may not have been lost – it might never have formed.

Exercise 6.2: Memories

Turn the radio on and listen to your favourite station. At the same time, please look at the picture on page 132 for a few minutes. If there is somebody with you, ask him or her to do the same. Then switch off and come back to this page.

Now, each of you take a piece of paper and write down everything you remember about what you saw and what you heard.

Consider how much detail each of you has written down. In fact a complete analysis, without deletion, would take an infinitely long time. There are several layers of information that we could unpack. Each part of the picture could be described in terms of the shapes and strokes. We could interpret its meanings to us, and the associations that it brings up. Similarly, the radio sounds could be decomposed into the various noises, instruments and voices, the combination of these into speech and musical pieces, with their meanings and associations for each of us. Then we could reflect on each other's associations...

Now refer again to page 132 and compare your notes with the picture. Many of the elements will seem distorted to you, because you didn't remember them that way. Interpretation can easily distort the meaning of what we experience.

If we think we understand something, we are likely to be mapping it across to something we already have in memory – a similar context, behaviour, thought, feeling or value. This is a process of generalisation – this must be like that. If we don't understand it, or we are asked to describe something that was too complex for us to describe to ourselves, we are likely to come up with a generalisation.

So, by the time it gets into memory, an experience has had a lot deleted, and has probably gone through considerable generalisation and distortion. This version of it makes it to unconscious memory, and can be recovered by questioning, association or the use of trance. Conscious memories are rather more complicated, because we add in other things that we have experienced (and deleted, distorted and generalised) before. These additions are edited to produce states, and our maps and models of the world, which are normally unconscious, but through which we interpret our experiences and memories.

Now we try to tell someone else what we have just witnessed. The conscious memory is now complicated and multi-layered. Associations have been added. We can only process a limited amount of information. Thus we again go through a process of deletion. We may have some outcome in view, perhaps to make ourselves look as good as possible, so we distort what we have seen to put ourselves in a better light. And in order to get across the essence of what we experienced, we generalise: "It was like being shown six films at the same time." In any case, we have no mechanism for getting across what we actually sensed. Our output is limited to our physiology, behaviours and words. If we want to discuss pictures, noises, tactile sensations, smells or tastes we can only use analogy – a process of generalisation.

Then what happens? The other person, the one we are trying to communicate with, only hears some of what we say, and only sees some of what we do. Then their internal filters cut in, and before it gets to their conscious memory, the experience has been further deleted, generalised and distorted.

So, if we need to get some vital information across, what do we do? We could just tell them and hope for the best, but then we are merely presupposing that they have remembered it. So, if it is important, we need to check that the information is available to them. Ask for feedback, possibly just a repetition of the message. It might be wise, though, to check that they act on the information in the way that you expect.

Exercise 6.3: Mimes

Let's have another game. Work in threes – a Model, an Instructor and an Observer. Each person should write down a job or role that can be *mimed*, that is, acted out without speaking. The idea is that an Observer will be able to say what the activity is. You should make the mime brief, but not too obvious: something that can be done without elaborate props or unusual skills.

The first Instructor tells the Model what the job or role is, without the Observer hearing it. The Model mimes the activity. The Observer tells the other two what he thinks the Model was asked to do. Then the Instructor demonstrates what she wanted doing and the Observer says what he thinks the Instructor's mime represented.

Briefly discuss the results, particularly any differences between what the Model did and what the Instructor demonstrated. Then change round – Observer to Model, Instructor to Observer, and repeat the exercise for each of the other two mimes.

Many of you seem surprised about what happened when you asked someone else to mime for you. It probably wasn't what you had imagined, or the sequence that you demonstrated. The instruction brought up different connections in your models of the world. And what did the Observers see? You knew that the actions of the mime were meant to represent something. Did the two demonstrations give you the same information, or point in different directions?

Consider your own mime. Let's take Paul's example – he asked his model to walk on to a zebra crossing, and just miss getting knocked down. When he instructed the Model, he deleted most of the detail about the way he wanted the scene to be played. Paul, judging by his demonstration, may have witnessed someone walking out without looking. Harry, who was the Model, seems to have been involved as a pedestrian, gesticulating at a driver whom he seems to blame. You each represented the scene from your own perceptual position, and distorted it to fit your own experience and values. The mime was of course generalised, because there was no road or zebra crossing, and no car. All it could do was fit generically.

Now shift to the role of Observer. You have three messages. You have seen Harry's mime, and Paul's mime, and you heard Paul's instructions to Harry. Each will bring up associations for you: they may be for the same or similar events, or for entirely different ones. The way that you interpret each message will depend on these associations.

119

Handout 6.1: Basic Fractal Language Model

Derivation of Model

Filter	Remedy	Process	Question
Deletion	Insert **Detail**	Adding	What?
Generalisation	Elicit boundaries & **Scope**	Extending	How?
Distortion	Establish **Connections**	Innovating	Why?

Fractal Language Model Patterns

Main	Sub-Levels		Pattern Type	Statement
Detail	Detail	Static	Components	I am worried.
		Dynamic	Comparatives	You are better.
	Scope	Static	Component References	Things are getting done late.
		Dynamic	Process-References	His work is better.
	Connections	Static	Lesser Nominalisations	She is busy.
		Dynamic	Nominalisations	We are in talks.
Scope	Detail	Static	Quantifiers	It's too much.
		Dynamic	Qualifiers	This is boring.
	Scope	Static	Static Scoping	People don't like you.
		Dynamic	Dynamic Scoping	Their troubles are increasing.
	Connections	Static	Modal Operator of Structure	We can't do it.
		Dynamic	Modal Operator of Sequence	I need a pay rise.
Connections	Detail	Static	Judgements/ Mind-reading	His wife doesn't like him.
		Dynamic	Injunctions/Lost Performative	Don't walk on the grass.
	Scope	Static	Complex Equivalence	Her grin means she has won.
		Dynamic	Concurrence/ Equation	He fell over and took the day off.
	Connections	Static	Inference	You smiled: you hate me.
		Dynamic	Cause-Effect	I lost the sale and I was sacked.

Vague or Hypnotic Language Pattern

Remove **Detail**

Extend boundaries and **Scope**

Make fallacious **Connections**

Clarifying Question	Process
Worried about what?	Add detail, be specific.
Compared to what?	Find out what the comparison is.
Such as what?	Limit the scope of the detail.
In what way?	Limit the scope of the comparison.
Doing what busily?	Make the adjective into an adverb.
What are you talking about?	Make the noun into a verb.
How much is too much?	Quantify the scope.
What about it is boring?	Limit the range of the scope.
Which people?	Get specific examples.
In what way?	Get more detail about an example.
What if you could do it?	Counter-example.
What if you didn't get one?	Look for consequences.
How do you know?	Find out how he came to the conclusion.
Who says?	Find the authority behind the injunction.
How do you know?	Look for evidence and question belief.
Is there any connection?	Question how the ideas fit together.
How do you conclude that?	Ask for evidence and thought patterns.
Did losing the sale lead to you being sacked?	Ask if these facts are connected.

In order to get the information we are given into a useful form, we only consider what we feel to be useful (deletion again), add and substitute references, experiences and analogies of our own (distortion and generalisation). This will happen every time we try to understand and report on external references.

Find out how some other people model the world, by trying this exercise as a party game, or a role-playing exercise at the office.

Language Models

Richard Bandler and John Grinder started to develop NLP in the early 1970s. One of their first aims was to restore some of the deletions and correct some of the generalisations and distortions in spoken communications so that they could make more sense *in their maps* of what was being said to them. Their two books on *The Structure of Magic* used work from linguistics, particularly the general semantics of Korzybski and the transformational grammar of Chomsky, to identify common patterns. They defined a set of questions to help to fill in the deleted material, and correct the distortions and generalisations. They called this the *Meta-model*. The patterns of deletions, generalisations and distortions are called Meta-model *violations*. A parallel system for deliberately introducing deletions, generalisations and distortions (for hypnotic and therapeutic purposes) was called the *Milton model*, after the noted hypnotherapist Dr Milton Erickson.

In the late 1980s, it was realised that these language models could be put into a single structure. The one we will look at is the *Basic Fractal Language Model*, devised by John McWhirter. This is outlined on Handout 6.1.

The purpose of a language model is to analyse the filtering processes that people are going through, and to recover information that has been filtered out.

The first distinction of the model is Detail. *Deletion* causes the loss of detail. Once we are aware of this, we can ask for more details to increase the information that we need. For example, if you say "I am concerned", I can ask you for more details by asking, "What are you concerned about?"

The second is labelled Scope. *Generalisation* is a process of losing boundaries or the scope of the information. Questions can be asked to re-establish the boundaries of the process – in response to the statement "People don't like me", you could ask, "Which people don't like you?"

Finally, the Basic Fractal Language Model deals with Connections. *Distortion* happens when you make inappropriate connections. You might connect things that are stated or include things that are not stated. The questioning process needs to investigate why connections have been made. Typical statements might be "I was late for work this morning and my boss sacked me this afternoon". You could ask, "Is there any connection between these events?" To the statement "He doesn't like me", you could respond, "How do you know that?" If the reply is "He is frowning", the question could be "How do you conclude that his frowning means that he doesn't like you?"

There are more language patterns than the three we have just heard about. John McWhirter suggested two additions. The first is to split each section as we split the epistemology grid – the what of the what, the how of the what, the why of the what, and so on. Thus we have the detail of the detail, the scope of the detail and the connections of the detail... The second is to divide the examples into static and dynamic ones. The lower part of Handout 6.1 shows the range of possibilities, and the names given in linguistic studies and in the Meta-model to the various patterns.

OK, so how do we use the Basic Fractal Language Model to improve our pacing and understanding of what others are saying? We are going to practise the patterns this afternoon, but let's just analyse some sentences using the patterns. We'll work with some professional content – the following are from recent advertisements. This will also give us a further chance to find pre-suppositions.

"BT's call prices – down, down and down again"

Presuppositions: That you know who BT is, you know what services it provides, and you are a customer or potential customer.
Detail: What kind of calls? (Detail) Down compared with what? (Scope) Whose calls to whom? (Connections)
Scope: Down by how much? (Detail) Are all call prices down? (Scope) What has to happen for call prices to be down? (Connections)
Connections: How do we know call prices are down? (Detail) Is there anything connected with call prices being down? (Scope) What can we infer from call prices being down? (Connections)

"Health Insurance. Cut the cost, not the cover."

Presuppositions: That you know what health insurance is, you know what it costs and covers, and you are someone who buys or might buy health insurance.
Detail: What kind of cover? (Detail) Cut the cost compared with what? (Scope) What are the costs and the cover? (Connections)
Scope: How much is the cut? (Detail) Which costs are cut? (Scope) What would happen if the costs were not cut? (Connections)
Connections: How do we know the cover is not cut? (Detail) Is the cover really health insurance? (Scope) Can we infer that we will get the same health care cover and cut our costs? (Connections)

"Seeking emotional and physical harmony? Try the detergents section of your local Sainsbury's."

Presuppostions: That you are seeking emotional and physical harmony; that you have a local Sainsbury's; that you can try its detergents section; that there is any point in trying it.
Detail: For what? (Detail) What kind of emotional and physical harmony? (Scope) Your harmonising with what? (Connections)
Scope: How much harmony? (Detail) Every local Sainsbury's? (Scope) What will happen if I don't? (Connections)
Connections: How do you know? (Detail) How will trying the detergent section of my local Sainsbury's help me to find emotional and physical harmony? (Scope) Is there any connection between seeking emotional and physical harmony and trying the detergents section of my local Sainsbury's? (Connections)

This is a good way to practise the language patterns – choose a few advertisements to practise on, or, for variety, some newspaper headlines. Try finding the presuppositions and questions for this one:

"Shareholders may gain vote on directors' pay"

We use language to evoke and describe sensations, memories, beliefs and values. We know that what we are being told includes presuppositions, and is incomplete, generalised and distorted, and we also know that in hearing it, we are adding our own presuppositions, reducing the detail, adding our own generalisations and further distorting the information. So how do we build on and correct the information that we are feeding into our internal model?

First we'll consider how to fill in the details of what we are being told. We will practise the Basic Fractal Language Model questions, and consider how to use Clean Language to ask about contexts, content and time orientation.

Exercise 6.4: Coaching
This is a multi-part exercise. Find a partner to work with, and then we'll take it in stages.

1.   Assume that you have an issue about the right way to do something. Take a few minutes to discuss these two questions: "Why don't you do it my way?" and "That's a good way to do it. Can you think how else it might be done?" Which would you prefer to say, and which would you prefer to hear?

Yes, most of you preferred the second question. The structure is to *match* the person's experience – "That's a good way to do it"– then to *pace* by asking them for more information: "Can you think how else it might be done?" If the person says "No", then you have the option to *lead* by offering another way to do it. OK.

2.   Now please assume you are in a work situation. Play the roles of Supervisor and Coach. As Supervisor, you have a subordinate who is doing a job inefficiently. Find a real, simple example from your own experience and share that with your Coach. Discuss with the Coach how you would make a difference to what is happening. Then change roles and repeat the exercise for the new Supervisor.

Let's find out how much you remember from the course so far. Did you all remember to get a *well-formed outcome*? Let's assume you decided to change the person's behaviour. If so, did you decide whether to change it by using behaviour, language and beliefs or feelings and values?

3.   Go back to the roles you were playing in Part 2. Take one Supervisor's example and discuss how to turn it into a well-formed outcome. Write down what you plan to do. Then do the same for the other example.

OK, can we hear one of these plans, please? PS, would you like to outline the situation?

"We have a boy in my office, Tim, who does lots of odd jobs. One of these is to photocopy all the documents that we need for sales visits. The problem is that he has no system. He'll pick up a set of originals and then leave it somewhere while he runs another errand, then come back with the wrong number of copies or pages missing. We decided that we would give him a system – that is, teach him the skill of following a set routine to do the copying properly. This would involve doing it at set times, with a form to fill in for each job. I would set up the system and supervise him, and I've set aside half a day next week to do it."

OK, that is a well-formed outcome, except that his actions are not under your control. Will he follow your system, or will he go back to his old ways? Can you think of ways to match and pace him so that he will make the changes for himself?

Let's have a demonstration. Would you come out to the front please, PS? I would like you to play the role of your office boy, and I will be the manager. As we go along *I will tell the group what I am doing.*

Now, Tim, you do the photocopying. The salesmen are wondering why it takes so long and sometimes comes back incomplete.

"I've got too much to do."

You say you have too much to do. What is it that takes up your time? *All the detail was deleted from the response, so we need to start getting some information.*

"Everybody keeps giving me jobs to do."

Everybody keeps giving you jobs to do? Could nobody else do the work? *Taking the generalisation and turning it round by asking another scope question.*

"Well, Susan seems to manage: she must work for a better group."

Susan manages the work: might it be the way she does it? *Challenging the implied cause-effect connection that Susan does her job because the group she works for is less demanding.*

"It might be."

Can you think of anything that you could do to make yourself less work? *We have determined that Tim thinks that he has too much to do. Now we are challenging him to set and achieve his own outcome, and satisfy his manager's outcome at the same time.*

Thank you, PS. We could continue this, by suggesting possibilities to him when he doesn't have any of his own. So, we'll continue with the exercise.

4.　　You have written plans to make a change. In your pairs, please do some role-playing as we have just demonstrated. The person with the plan should be the Subordinate, while your partner is the Manager. The Manager should put the behavioural difficulty to the Subordinate, and find out the *details*, *scope* and *connections*. Then lead into getting the Subordinate to accept your plan as his or her own outcome.

OK, I can see that was quite complicated the first time through. Some of you got stuck by finding out all sorts of details, and your challenges took you away from the outcome you were after. This will need practice. You might start by running through one of these interviews on paper, writing down the Manager's questions and the Subordinate's responses. Get the feel of where the various questions lead you.

Beliefs

As you went through that last exercise, you might have noticed how many of the responses you got were in the form of beliefs. Many of you will have heard "I'm too busy" or "I don't know how to do that". In this section, we are going to work with beliefs that are in the language that we use. These may be hidden linguistic formulations, or directly marked as beliefs or knowledge.

In order to pace people, you will need to find out what they believe, and how those beliefs fit into their model. In this context, presuppositions, beliefs and identity statements are equivalent. Most sentences will include at least a presupposition.

If someone uses the verb 'to be', they are almost always showing a belief. Let's have some examples:

"I am here" – presupposes a *here* (may not be obvious on the phone).
"You are good" – a belief (may or may not be true, and the detail is missing).
"She is a writer" – an identity statement (may need to be interpreted).

Similarly, most sentences with a *modal operator* – e.g. can, must, should, want, like, need – include beliefs. For example:

"You can wait" – presupposes that I am willing and able to wait.

"We need books" – the reason for the need is presupposed.

"He should succeed" – a belief that he can and will succeed.

"They like us" – a belief: simple mind-reading unless we have evidence.

Statements including a *universal quantifier* – e.g. always, never, every, no one, all, none, people – generally include beliefs, often easily falsifiable ones. Try:

"It always falls that way" – does it always fall that way?

"No one believes me" – does no one believe you, ever?

"I have none" – may need testing.

"The sun rises every day" – a type of identity statement.

Listen for *comparatives* and *superlatives*: these often indicate beliefs, especially if there is no direct comparison:

"We do more" – more than what?

"He works better than Jones" – can we test that?

"The least cost solution" – who says so?

"Choose the brighter picture" – which do you believe is brighter?

The Basic Fractal Language Model *Connections* patterns are all about beliefs. They are marked by words like 'know', 'means' or 'equals'; direct orders or judgements; and sentences where there are two separate ideas. Examples are:

"She let me down" – how do you know?

"Do it now!" – equivalent to "I believe that you will do it if I tell you to."

"Waiting means losing the contract" – what evidence is there?

"He smiles and I feel threatened" – what do you believe that he will do?

"My head aches because of what you said" – why do you believe that?

"Boys make him show off" – whose belief is that, yours or his?

And don't forget that you might hear "I believe that", "I know that", "I consider that" or "I identify myself with".

Exercise 6.5: Noticing Beliefs

Let's practise *noticing beliefs*. Think of a skill you have in some family or leisure activity. Get into pairs, Coach and Client. Alternatively, you could tape-record the statement and analyse it yourself.

The Coach asks the Client to talk about her skill, allowing the Coach to write down what is said. Next to the statement, note any presuppositions, beliefs and identity statements that you hear. Continue until you have filled the page.

Then the Coach and Client should get together and analyse what has been written. Add in any further beliefs that you find, and note which beliefs the Client considers to be positive, and which negative. The Coach should remain neutral – use Clean Language questions if you wish to clarify anything.

Take about 15 minutes, then change roles and repeat the exercise.

You all noticed plenty of presuppositions, beliefs and identity statements, and found some that you regarded as positive or *resourceful*, and some as negative or *unresourceful*. There will be quite a number, especially presuppositions, which do not carry any emotional charge for you – they either seem to be statements of fact, or the way that you normally speak. These may be the ones that give the listener the best insight into your model of the world.

The resourceful beliefs are probably the reason that you have the skill that you were talking about. Believing that you are good at something takes you quite a long way towards being good at it. Of course it could just be self-delusion, but you would normally have some evidence to back it up.

Unresourceful beliefs are a means by which you limit yourself. This limiting may be useful. If you know you are bad at driving a car, you are more likely to take some lessons before you go out on the road. Sometimes, though, we are unconsciously stopping ourselves from doing things that in fact we can or could do. If you say to yourself, "I can't use a computer" before you learn how to do it, you are limiting yourself without any good reason.

It is worth using this method of checking for beliefs to find out what are *your* unnecessary areas of weakness: problems, things you can't do well or wouldn't try. Doing the exercise by yourself on paper means that you don't have to tell anyone else what these problems used to be.

Before we go any further, does anyone have anything they'd like to share about beliefs they have calibrated: Amanada?

> "Yes, do you remember I told you on Day One that my out-
> come is to make a hit record, singing with my boyfriend
> and his band? Well, I saw him about it during the week,
> showed him my notes about language and beliefs. We
> decided to tape a conversation about wanting to make the
> record, so that I could analyse it afterwards. What I found
> was that we were both keen, but we wondered whether to
> take the risk. We both believed that we are good, though. So
> we looked at the proposition, bearing in mind how well our
> last gig went, and we have booked a recording studio for
> the weekend."

Excellent, Amanada, you must tell us how it all turns out.

Today, you have let your minds wander through all you know about pacing, bearing in mind the details of the language that people are using when they talk to you. Your outcomes have become better structured and informed by what you know, in your unconscious mind as well as your thoughts. The information will be available to you when you need it.

The constant theme of this course is that the more you practise, the more automatic these tools will be in use. Now you have the skills to go out and find better ways to practise, and in learning from others you will learn better how to do it for yourself. In particular, this week, notice the language patterns that people are using while you talk to them. Track their beliefs if conditions allow. And spend some time finding out what your beliefs are in particular contexts.

So, enjoy all that learning and doing. Have a wonderful exper-ience of discovery, and come back next time to learn all about values systems.

Homage to MCE

Day Seven:
Sets of Values

I hope that you have found time to practise the techniques you learned last time. Today we are going to find out more about pacing *internal states* – values, feelings and emotions – and finding out how people respond to particular words and situations. This is what we are going to cover this time:

• *Beliefs and Values*
Beliefs are internal processes, formed and expressed in language. *Values* are internal states that include both linguistic (this is important to me) and emotional components.

• *Internal States*
Internal states can be linked to what we sense, think or remember. Situations (particularly one that remind us of strong emotions) and *semantically dense* words can act as *triggers* and take us into the states that are *anchored* to them.

• *Processing Preferences*
Some linguistic patterns can trigger positive or negative responses in relatively neutral situations. As an example, you can test how you react to the amount of detail people use when they are speaking to you. Some people prefer the *global picture*, with big concepts and little detail. Others are happier to know all the concrete *small details*.

• *Pacing States*
Pacing states means finding out what is going on inside another person – how he is feeling, what he values and how he is likely to react to a situation or form of words. You will learn how to recognise what people *value*, where they attend, how they *choose* and whether they normally move *towards* or *away from* things. You will consider your own values in connection with *money*, and look at some categories in which you could categorise money values.

Just by noticing what you value about the things that you believe, you can increase the choices that you have. And you made sure that the decisions felt right to you, as well.

Yes, Apricot?

"Thank you. I was talking to my assistant about a new sales brochure he is working on. I told him that it didn't look very exciting to me. He muttered something about trying his best and feeling OK about it. His tone struck me as not being very congruent, so I checked with him whether there was anything wrong. It came out eventually that he didn't believe the new options that we were offering were good value for money. He couldn't see anyone wanting to buy them, so he was rather disheartened about trying to provide a sales pitch.

"Well, he is quite experienced, so I did some research. He was right – the surveys we'd done didn't show any great enthusiasm for the options. We do need the sales from them to meet our budget targets next year. So I called a couple of customers who had been shown the original proposal, and asked what they'd really want. The board are going to discuss some alternatives in the next few days."

Thank you, Apricot. Here we have beliefs driving both feelings and behaviour. A perceived limitation – that your assistant wasn't doing a good job with the leaflet – has been turned into an opportunity to improve the product.

Beliefs and Values

I can hear from your feedback that there is still some confusion about the definition of values and how they are distinguished from beliefs. Remember that believing is an internal *process* – beliefs can be analysed using language, and reasons given for them. Values and other internal *states* may well include beliefs, but they also have an emotional or physiological component.

You might hear a statement: "Running is good for you." If you are unsure whether this reflects a belief or a value, then ask: "How do you know running is good for you?" If it is a belief, you will get an answer along the lines of "It has been proved..." whereas with a value the reply will be more like "Because it feels good". Often, you will get both kinds of answer, showing that the belief forms part of a value. Another frequent type of response involves an incongruity between beliefs and values. "I know that running is good for, me but I don't like doing it." The two statements will be separated by a word such as 'but', 'however' or 'though', and there will probably be a change in physiology.

I have been getting some questions about how these techniques can be used in normal life. There is a worry that you will be seen as trying to control other people. You are getting to be more skilled in noticing and picking up what people say and why they are saying it. We haven't yet gone into much detail about leading them – that will start next time. You know it is possible. You know it is also possible to lead, teach and control them in all sorts of other ways – for example: bribery, punishment, or advertising. Any leading you do is under the control of your conscience, your values. The techniques in this course do nothing to change those for the worse.

Some of you are concerned that you will harm relationships if you use the techniques, especially if you get them 'wrong'. Just bear in mind that all we have done so far is to learn to listen better, and help the person we are in conversation with give us a fuller account of their model of the situation. Anything we do towards that outcome will be beneficial. If what you are doing seems to be unhelpful, then do something different. In particular, if your questioning seems harsh and directive, make it softer by physiological rapport, using their predicates and repeating back more of their words. Keep your questions as clean as possible.

Yes, it can be difficult to remain conscious of all the things that you should be doing. Don't try. Practise each part separately until you know it unconsciously. The more you do it, the easier it becomes.

Let's do some more work on states, feelings and values. In particular, you will learn how to be in the right state to achieve your outcome, or to get someone else into the mood to listen to your proposition.

Internal States

Our internal states are driven by what we sense, the words we hear and our thoughts and memories. Probably memory is where states are formed. Once we have reacted to a particular trigger with a singular response, we are more likely to do the same in the future. This is the basis of learning, habits, values, morality and what we might call our personality profile.

A state can be anchored to any of the [VAKOGD] senses – pictures, sounds, touches, smells, tastes and words, in any combination. Sometimes the trigger event can be quite complex. Evoking a fear of flying might mean visualising the inside of an aircraft, hearing the noises, feeling the change in air pressure, telling yourself "It's going to crash", and visualising the burning wreckage on the ground.

Getting into your most resourceful state for speaking to a large audience might include telling yourself that you know all the material. Tell yourself that they are really going to appreciate your contribution. Visualise a happy, applauding audience and have a warm glow inside. Then give yourself a fanfare with which to walk on to the stage.

When you are communicating, you need to pace the person you are working with to find out what some of her triggers and anchored states are. There will be words that trigger a change in her state.

Some of these work for most people, others are very personal. These are called semantically dense words.

Before we start working on states, it is a good idea to have a good state to return to at any time. I suggest that we install the State of Curiosity and Wonder (Exercise 4.5).

Worksheet 7.1: Semantic Density

Client	Coach
WORD	**STATE EVOKED**
Gun	
Baby	
Hope	
Home	
Idiot	
Holiday	
Lesson	
Cool	
God	
Cat	

Failure	
Fire	
Smart	
Please	
Warm	
Lover	
Travel	
Lottery	
Diet	
Mother	

139

Exercise 7.1: Words that Change States

OK, we are ready to start finding out what sensations, feelings, emotions, thoughts and beliefs come to mind when we hear or see various words with semantic density for us. So get into pairs, Coach and Client, and take Worksheet 7.1.

The Coach should read out the first of the twenty words in the list. Notice how the Client reacts physiologically. Note any verbal reaction. Then ask what state the Client is in. Enquire whether the Client is making any representations, and note any belief or value statements. Clarify anything you are uncertain about. Once that is all recorded, ask the Client to get back into State of Curiosity and Wonder.

Continue down the list. When you have notes on the first ten words, change over, re-establish the state of curiosity and wonder, and continue with the second ten words for the new Client.

Any surprises there? Yes, several of you found that the reaction of the Coach and Client to a particular word were very different. Circumstances can make a considerable difference: the word 'Baby' might produce different states in a mother who had been up all night with a teething infant; a teenage boy waiting for news from his girlfriend; and a couple in the waiting room of a fertility clinic. Experience will also play its part. Those of you who found learning fun will have one reaction to 'Lesson' – those who hated school might have a different one. Other states may be individual: I don't want to pry into what lies behind the state that Prudence experienced when offered 'Warm'. And I noticed the clear indications of love, hate and neutrality generated by the word 'Cat'.

All this shows that you need evidence before you can be certain whether words will trigger states in other people – your own map is unlikely to be a good guide. Go out and notice what happens when you use semantically dense words to people in conversation, but be careful out there – some words can trigger very powerful emotions. It is important to notice how your conversation partner is attending when you are speaking. They are more likely to react if they are associating fully in the first person, rather than second-positioning you, or being completely dissociated from the scene.

Processing Preferences

People don't just change state in response to particular words. They will have different ways of looking at the world, and sets of automatic responses to situations. These will trigger positive or negative states depending on the individual's *processing preferences* in that context. For example, some people prefer to talk about the big picture, while others like small details. These preferences may be fixed, or depend on the context. In a discussion about cars, we might be talking about the shape of hubcaps, differences between 1.6-litre hatchbacks or the future of road transport policy. Each context will require different levels of detail. Some people are happier with small, concrete details – colours, measurements and comparisons. Others are comfortable with the global picture – world trends, philosophical arguments and sweeping generalisations.

Exercise 7.2: Preferences for Detail

Get together in pairs, Coach and Client, to try out the effect of talking at different levels of detail. Find enough space to establish a line several paces long. Mark the *Small Detail* position on the Client's right and *Global Picture* on the left.

The Client should stand behind the line to start with. Talk for a few minutes about a task that you do at work.

The Coach should then take the Client to stand at the Small Detail position and talk about the same task for a few more minutes. The Coach should encourage the Client to go into more and more detail. Briefly discuss the Client's state.

Next, the Coach should take the Client to stand at the Global Picture position and talk about the same task. This time the Coach should lead the Client to talk about the philosophy, overview and consequences of the task. Again, briefly discuss the Client's state.

Now ask the Client to walk along the line, continuing to talk about the task. Match the level of detail in the statement to the position on the line. Go to the Small Detail position, and then walk back to Global Picture.

Ask the Client to stand at a number of positions on the line, and consider what contexts would suit that level of detail, and what appropriate states would be.

Change roles, and repeat the exercise for the new Client.

What are the effects of being at the 'wrong' level of detail? Imagine planning the local fête if you are not allowed to mention details like places, times or amounts. And imagine discussing the history of ideas if you could only talk about objects, shapes and angles. Now feel what it is like when someone is speaking to you at the 'wrong' level of detail. Some of us feel irritated, frustrated or angry. Others may just 'turn off'.

Small Detail Position

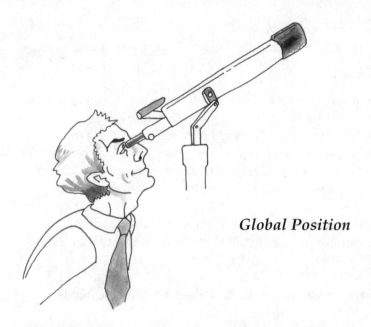

Global Position

There are many processing preferences. Studies have found more than eighty sets of what NLP calls Meta-programs. If you notice someone using a particular pattern, try to match and pace it. The more flexible we can be in pacing other people's processing preferences, the better we will be at communicating.

Pacing States

Let's just remind ourselves of the types of state that we might have to pace. We looked at underlying emotional states on Day Four. You can pace simple feelings like happiness or depression largely from physiology. Just notice the state changes. We have just learned about reactive state changes caused by semantically dense language and processing preferences.

More complex states tend to be called *values* or *personality traits*. These are much more fixed in nature, although a person may only show particular values in a given context. Values are the things that are important to people. We learned to elicit values and put them into hierarchies on Day Four. For pacing purposes, though, we may not want to ask direct questions. Can we find a way to pick up values from the conversation?

Exercise 7.3: Pacing Values

Work in pairs, Model and Pacer. The Pacer should take notes on Worksheet 7.2.

Ask the Model to speak about an important part of her job for a few minutes. Listen for clues about what her values are. Notice whether her attention is directed to herself, to others or on ideas or things. Hear whether her action criteria are based on beliefs or feelings, and what is important about them. Get a feeling for what she is moving towards and away from.

Once you have some notes under most of the headings, discuss the results, and find out whether the Model agrees that these are her work values.

Then change roles and note the values for the new Model.

You could find out about what you say about your own values in other contexts. Tape-record and analyse a statement on a significant subject – say, about your family, hobby or personal development.

Did you all find that you could pick up a number of values just by listening to your partner? If his conversation doesn't include values, you can give some direction by asking about things that are important while he is doing the job.

In everyday life, we do make judgements about how people will behave. We describe them as outgoing, sad, preoccupied or driven. Psychologists put people into types – introvert or extrovert, blamer, placator or distracter, manic or depressed. We have also learned to match our conversation partners' physiology and behaviour, their language and beliefs. How much might this tell us about their processing preferences?

Worksheet 7.2: Values

	Direction	Examples
Attention		
Inwards to self		
Outwards to others		
On ideas or things		
Choice		
On the basis of doing something		
On the basis of believing something		
On the basis of feeling something		
Action		
Proactive, towards feeling good about something		
Reactive, away from feeling bad about something		

If you are going to guess, from the evidence you have, how some-one else will react, then this is a presupposition. You will need to test it, and you will need to have a strategy in place to pace the person if you are wrong. So be ready to accept all the feedback that you are offered. Remember what you have discovered. If your pac-ing goes astray, then revert to matching: use their physiology, behaviours, predicates, beliefs and words.

If the person you are communicating with is someone you know well, then you are probably aware, at least unconsciously, of some of their values. Instinctively, you will probably know what to say to pace them. The difficulty may come in remembering to match and pace, especially if you habitually mismatch them.

With people you don't know well, one strategy might be to try analogy. You could make the assumption that this person will react like someone else you know. It will not, of course, be true. People are not carbon copies of each other. But there may be enough sim-ilarity to help you pace your communicating while you learn more about their model of the world.

At a more abstract level, you might keep a set of responses to par-ticular personality types and contexts. This is where the social or psychological models might come into play. Again, these are stereotypes. Nobody will actually be identical to the model. However, if I give you a context and a type of person, you would have some idea of how to play the role. This role is a basis to start matching and pacing values.

We have learned examples of these roles in all kinds of ways. We have unconsciously learned about people we know, and people we have read about or seen in films or on the television. You will have some idea of how your role model behaves, what he believes and what he values.

Exercise 7.4: Playing a Role

We can all do this together. Stand up. You are a traffic cop. The car you have stopped was doing 20 miles an hour over the speed limit. Go over and talk to the driver.

Good, sit down again. Now let's find out what values we were assuming in order to do that exercise. Where was your *attention*? You were focused mainly on *others* – on the driver and on road users he might have put at risk. Part of your attention was directed to *ideas* – the law, safe driving and doing your duty. *Beliefs* were probably more important than *feelings* – the concentration was on facts, actions and regulations. How you personally felt about speeding shouldn't have come into it. Your actions were essentially *reactive* – the driver was speeding and you stopped him. You were moving *away from* lawbreaking, perhaps *towards* road safety.

Now play the scene again, this time taking the role of the speeding motorist. Sit in your car waiting for the constable to come and speak to you. Now he is at the window. Hear what is said, and imagine how you would feel.

Did you match and pace the police officer, or did you try to lead from the beginning? Which do you think would be the more effective strategy? Did you find an effective state to use for the interview? Imagine that you were matching and pacing him. Was an awareness of his job values useful in carrying on the conversation? Would knowing anything about his other values have helped?

Exercise 7.5: Money Values

Now let's look at another context for values: money. Work individually to start with – take a piece of paper and write down at least five statements in response to "What is important to you about money?" You might want to think about earning, spending, saving, taxing, accounting, ignoring, investing, borrowing, lending, winning, losing, giving, inheriting, hoarding and wasting.

OK, you have a big stack of statements amongst you. Let's put them into some categories.

Do we have any values that suggest that money is a magic topic – something that can't be understood? Yes, a number of you would like to ignore it, don't understand it or account for it. Money comes and goes, and probably someone in the family has some if you need it.

Next, can we hear about values that equate money with *power*? You have a right to money – earn it, steal it or borrow it. Spending is of secondary importance: the important thing is to have it. If there is any about, it's mine, and I'll fight you for it.

The next group of values includes *rules* to do with money. You earn the rate for the job, keep up-to-date accounts, save for a rainy day, never a borrower nor a lender be, protect your investments, and want something to leave to your children.

Now we come to the *entrepreneurial* statements about money. These are values about making money work, taking calculated risks, making profits, borrowing to take advantage of the market, earning a good return on capital, enjoying a good lifestyle.

There are those who concentrate on the *social* values of money. These will include earning money to use for others, charity, sharing and co-operation, ethical investment, stake holding, community projects and fair taxation.

Finally, you have generated some statements that treat money as part of a *system*. Key words include tool, token or proxy: money is seen as useful, a means to an end, a way of keeping score, only part of the picture.

These are very different ways of looking at money. Try taking your most important money value, and fitting it into each of these categories. Can we have an example, please? Thank you, Stephen. Your value is "I want to save enough for a good retirement income".

The *magic* version of this is "There will be some money around when we want to retire". The *power* value might be "If I get some money I won't need to work". Another *rule* could say "You can't retire until you have enough savings". The *entrepreneurial* variation might be "Once I've made enough money I'll do something different". A *social* approach might be "When there's enough money to go round, we can concentrate on voluntary work". The *systems* formulation could be "My activities will change depending on the balance between my interests, cash flow and other outcomes".

Exercise 7.6: Trying on Values

Work in pairs, Model and Coach. Write out each of the value types on a separate piece on paper: *Magic, Power, Rules, Entrepreneur, Social* and *Systems*. Lay these pieces of paper out on the floor in whatever position you find useful. Agree a context that you are going to work with.

The Model should take on the State of Curiosity and Wonder. The Coach should take the Model to each of the positions in turn, and ask the Model to go into the context with the values system in that position. Find out the state that each one triggers. Some will be more comfortable than others. While you are in the state, consider how you would match and pace someone with that system of values.

Once the Model has experienced each value type, change roles and repeat the exercise for the new Model.

Some of you were very surprised when you took on the unfamiliar values. Would someone like to talk us through the experience? Thank you, Apricot.

> "The context we chose was deciding on a holiday. *Magic* took me to memories of Guide camps and pop festivals. There is a feeling of irresponsibility, with someone else taking all the decisions. You can't really decide anything in this position – the feeling is going with the flow. *Power* made me think of what I really want to do. I could ignore everyone else and do something very selfish. Perhaps I should take up snowboarding or get up early at the resort and throw all the German tourists' towels into the swimming pool.

"*Rules* reminded me of a week at a holiday camp, where there is a time and place for everything, and the menu is always the same. You meet people there that have booked the same week in the same chalet for twenty years. *Entrepreneur* is my usual values system. I'm willing to pay for what I want, and I'm going to have a good time. I'll take a few risks doing new things and have some excitement.

"*Society* brought to mind rather earnest, working holidays. I see conservation weekends, workshops on the advance of socialism and lecture tours: people being polite and co-operative, but not having fun. It might be all right if you were part of a team with the right purpose. *Systems* – you have to have a system that gets you to book the time off and arrange to go. It made me think why I want a holiday, and how it fits in with the other things I am doing.

"I can see that people with those values systems would have very different reactions when you talk about holidays. If I were selling holidays, I'd have to talk to each of them appropriately. I just hope that I would notice quickly enough what their values were."

To get some more practice, monitor some conversations that you hear around you, or on radio or television. Pace the values that you hear being expressed, and try some of them on for size. Notice what happens in discussions where the participants have different values systems. Listen to political arguments or wage negotiations. What do you think would happen if the participants could find a common system of values?

As the saying goes, things work when we put body and soul into them. We get the best results by behaving in a particular way and having the appropriate thoughts and feelings to go with what we are doing. Jobs get done if we are enthusiastic about them. We make good decisions if we get the point of them.

Just look back for a moment on all that you have learned in the last seven weeks. Now look forward to that point where you have succeeded in using them all to improve that special communication that you had to get right. Just feel how valuable it has been to become competent in these techniques that you can now use automatically.

So, next week, you will begin to find out how to lead in your communicating, and how to use your words to change behaviour.

Day Eight:
Directing Behaviour

We are now ready to investigate how to *lead* in communicating with other people, to get them to change what they do. The next two sessions will concentrate on getting people to change how they think and feel. The main lessons for today are:

● *Doing It Better*

First we will examine some working behaviours that we want to change. Then you will decide where and how to intervene and set up well-formed outcomes. You may choose to *do* something to change the behaviour, use *language* skills or change the person's *feelings* about the job.

● *Adding Creativity*

What if you can't think of any way of making the change? You will work through the *Disney Creativity Pattern*. This allows you to generate dream or fantasy solutions, turn them into workable plans and check them for effectiveness. We will discuss how you might set up a system at the office.

● *Leading Skills*

When you have decided on your outcome, and you have matched and paced the person you want to work with, you have to decide what kind of *lead* to use. You could set rules, teach or coach. We will have an exercise on leading as a coach.

● *Directing Effort*

You may want to move people who are not subordinates – your bosses, friends or a group of customers. We will try out some ideas to get them to change what they do by pacing their beliefs.

● *Influencing Activity*

A powerful way of getting someone to change their behaviour is to appeal to their feelings and values. If we make something *important* enough, it will get done.

● *Leading Conversations*

When do you stop *pacing* and start *leading*? That is a skill, one that we have learned from childhood. Using your skills of *rapport* and *calibration*, you should be able to tell when your lead is being accepted and when it isn't. If the lead doesn't work, you go back to matching and pacing. *Directive language* is a lead that gets someone to do something for you.

Before we go on, we'll have another look at your *action outcomes*. Sir John, you have a point?

> "Yes. When we have been setting our well-formed outcomes, we have had to assume that the outcome must be in our control. Now we are going on to talk about changing what other people do, should we be relaxing this condition? For a lot of what I need to achieve for Whizzitts Ltd, I need to get the co-operation of my managers and staff."

As we said in the first session, if your outcome depends on other people, then you need to have contingency plans in case they do not react as you expect. Using the techniques that you will be taught in this session, you may be able to increase the chances of your managers and staff doing what you expect them to, but it would be wise to arrange some fallback options. Don't forget that outcome-setting is a process, a series of steps; it is not an end in itself.

Doing It Better

In this session, we are looking at changing behaviour. We can lead others through behaviour, using thoughts or beliefs, or by suggesting feelings. Each of these channels for change has a range of uses, and we will be discussing what use each might be, and some techniques for making changes.

Exercise 8.1: Behavioural Outcomes

Let's start by writing down some items of *behaviour* that you want to change in other people. There is no limit to the context – they could be workmates or bosses, family or friends, or just people you have to deal with. On Worksheet 8.1 write down their name or job title, what they do "wrong", and what you would prefer them to do. Take five minutes and write down as many as you can – at least half a dozen.

Worksheet 8.1:   *Adding Skills*

Name/Title	Behaviour	Desired Change	Method
1			
2			
3			
4			
5			
6			
7			
8			
9			
10			

OK, let's hear some examples of what you have come up with. It might help to separate them by context, so we will begin with the ones to do with working with subordinates – what we might call *supervising*. You might prefer to use pseudonyms or job descriptions rather than real names, and just give us a few words about the behaviour. Apricot, would you like to begin?

> "Yes. There is a secretary in my office who smokes when he thinks no one will notice. That is against company policy and unpleasant for the rest of us. I want him to stop."

That is a common experience. Please remember that these outcomes need to be well formed. How can we put that in the positive? Perhaps by saying that you want him to work in the office and smoke during breaks outside the office? OK. Now what ways do you have available to achieve that outcome?

You could start with the *environmental framing*. Check that there are times and places where he could smoke. Check that he actually wants to smoke – he might like to give up entirely with the right help. Check that he wants to work in your department, or whether smoking in the office is just a way of getting you to dismiss or move him.

So, he is going to go on working with you, and you want him to follow your rules. How might you change his behaviour *behaviourally*? One possibility is to threaten punishment. No doubt you have a misconduct code, and you could use it, give him formal warnings and eventually sack him. Another way might be a kind of aversion therapy. I am not recommending this, but it might be possible to have an office junior follow him around the office with a bucket of water. When he lights up, pour the water over him. I'm sure you could think of less drastic ways of acting.

Now, how might you change his behaviour *cognitively* – changing the way he thinks and what he believes? You might use argument, telling him the effect smoking is having on his health or on other people's clothes. You would have to get inside his model of the world and change the part where he believes that smoking in the office is a good idea.

Finally, how might you change his behaviour *emotionally* – changing his behaviour by working on his feelings? You could use fear – of ill health, ostracism or dismissal. You might use friendship – persuade him that people would like him better if he did not smoke in the office. Work within his model of the world, find out what drives him, and use that to change his behaviour.

So, you have a number of possible approaches. I would always recommend starting with the context and environment, to check that you are trying to make a sensible and appropriate change. Then you have a range of choices about how to intervene and lead.

Let's have another example – one where you are trying to get someone at the same level or senior to you to behave differently. We might call this *co-operating*. Yes, all right, we will take the obvious one. What do you do if you want to stop your boss smoking in your office?

OK. First review everything we said about stopping your secretary from smoking. Consider the *context* and environmental issues. Does he want to give up smoking? Is he trying to give you some other message, possibly about power, or about your position in the company? You will need to pay a lot of attention to your outcome, in particular what you can start and maintain. Be aware of the resources that you have and take care with the ecology checks.

You could *behave* in the same ways as we outlined in the last case. An appeal to the rules might have some effect if her superiors are willing to enforce them – but what will that do to your working relationship? The same might apply to the bucket of water technique. The techniques for changing behaviour through *language* and *feelings* will be very similar to the case of the secretary. The language you use to make the changes might be different, and you would be wise to be quite certain that you are working within her model of the world.

We have seen that the *context* and the environment are very important considerations. We may not need or want to make changes to the person that we are dealing with. It might be easier or necessary to make other kinds of change. If someone is annoying you, do you want to change their behaviour, or can you just keep them away from you? Are there changes you need to make in yourself rather than in others? How else could you make a difference to the situation?

Adding Creativity

Many of you will have used brainstorming techniques such as those devised by Edward de Bono and Tony Buzan. Today, I am going to introduce you to a method that was devised by Robert Dilts. Walt Disney and his team encouraged creativity in the production of their animated films. They realised that the process of getting and developing an idea had three phases – the original *dreaming*, the *planning* you go through to achieve it, and the process of *critiquing* the plans to turn them into well-formed outcomes. Disney separated these functions physically, so that he had separate work areas for them. The dream room was like an artist's studio, the planning room was like an office, and the critiquing area was functional.

When Robert Dilts was putting the Disney Creativity Pattern together, he realised that people play a different role in each phase and they behave, think and feel differently in each role. The pattern involves setting aside areas for each role, and anchoring the appropriate state in each place. He also added a Meta-position from which you can study the whole process.

We are all going to practise this pattern together. The details are on Worksheet 8.2. Each corner of this room will be one of the role-playing positions. Going round clockwise, that corner is for dreaming, the next for planning, that one for critiquing, and the last is a Meta-position. Can you all please move into the *dreaming* corner?

OK. Please think of a time when you were really creative and open to considering new things. You had lots of ideas and could really see the pictures of what you were thinking about. Really get into the way you felt then: see what you saw, hear what you heard, feel what was happening to you, and be there. Good, most of you are adopting a visualising posture – standing upright, eyes up, nice smile, really opening up to the possibilities that are coming to you. Anchor that state to this location.

Good. Now move to the *Meta-position*. See yourself in the dreaming corner, really being creative.

Next we are going to stand in the *realist*, or *planning*, space. In this corner, remember a time when you were really planning well. You were on top of the situation, and could list everything that needed doing. Get into that role, hear yourself giving the instructions, see what you could see and feel what you felt. Yes, I see most of you are in an auditory position – as if you were talking on the phone or to a colleague. Anchor that planning state to this space.

OK. Move back to the Meta-position and see and hear yourself in the planning space, putting together a really good plan.

Now we will set up the *overview*, or *critiquing*, section. Here, I would like you to remember times when you helped someone else to critique their plans, and made useful suggestions to improve them. You knew when those plans were ready to be put into action. There was a particular feeling in your body, and perhaps a word, sound or picture that confirmed that it was right. Get into that state, feel those feelings, hear what was said, see what you saw. Yes, it is a matter of gut feel. Anchor that state of helping to improve the plan in this space.

Right, come back the Meta-position again. You can see, hear and feel yourself in each of the other roles.

Exercise 8.2: Creating New Options

Now we can work on a particular outcome to practise the Disney Pattern. Take one of the examples from Worksheet 8.1 where you have yet to find enough options for achieving the change. Work in pairs, Explorer and Coach. The Explorer is going to create new choices for achieving change, and the Coach will guide the Explorer through the pattern, using Worksheet 8.2. Use the positions in the room that we have just set up.

The Coach does not need to be told any of the details of what is happening. Just calibrate the Explorer to check that each process has been completed before you move on to the next one.

Worksheet 8.2:   *Disney Creativity Pattern*

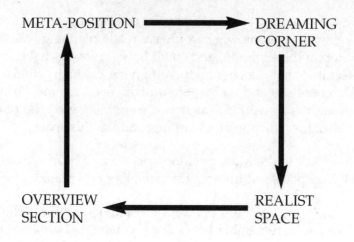

Setting Up

1. Anchor the 'creative' state in dreaming corner, the 'planning' state in the realist space, and the 'critiquing' state in the overview section.

2. Review each state from the Meta-position.

Using Disney Creativity

1.   Go to the dreaming corner. Ask the Explorer to get into the dreamer role, and visualise as many ways of achieving the change as possible. They do not have to be practical or possible. Make movies of how these methods might work. See yourself carrying them out.

2.   Go to the realist space. Ask the Explorer to get into the role, and consider how to add detail to achieve your outcomes.

3.   Go to the overview section. Ask the Explorer to get into the role, and think through the plans, looking for constructive ways they can be improved.

4.   Go to the meta-position. Using the information that you have gathered, consider what else you have to create to achieve the change.

5.   Go to the dreaming corner and state. Visualise the improved dreams, then take them through the other three positions. If more needs to be added, continue round again. Once you are happy with the plans, go to the dreaming corner for a final time, and experience what it will be like to have achieved your desired outcome.

6.   Once the first Explorer has been through the pattern, switch roles and repeat the exercise. Take about 20 minutes per person.

It looks as if there are some extremely satisfactory results there. Are there any questions? Yes, in a practical situation, you might want to add all sorts of physical resources to the three role-playing positions. In the dreaming section, you might want things to help you to visualise better and make more pictures. You would probably also need ways of recording the pictures, and accessing other people's pictures. In the planning space, you would need plans in writing, and all the tools to do the research – laboratories, workshops and libraries. The critiquing space might be a boardroom table or a group gathered round the coffee machine. Or you might just be able to do the whole process in your head. It depends on the scale of the outcome that you are working on.

Leading Skills

How do we make a change behaviourally? We *do* something that makes a difference to someone else. We might offer tangible rewards or punishments. We could demonstrate what to do, or show them what is being done wrongly. It might be necessary to bring in a teacher, or we might find that the person already has the skill, but has to be reminded to use it.

Exercise 8.3: Deciding on a Lead
Get into pairs, and take your Worksheet 8.1. Discuss each of your examples. Between you, decide how a change in the *environment*, the relationship or in yourself would provide a satisfactory outcome. Then decide how you would make a change by *doing* something, how you can make the change by using *language* and beliefs, and how you can work on the outcome through *feelings* and values.

Make sure that you have at least two good examples each of environmental, behavioural, cognitive and emotional changes. Then use the Disney Creativity process to work out how you might intervene in these cases.

Can we all hear about some of the changes you want to make to behaviour by doing something? Stephen, you have something from the production area?

> "Yes. Sometimes I have the problem of people working too slowly. I can see that they know how to do the task, and their attitude seems to be generally OK. But if one slows down it is infectious. You can see the energy drop from bay to bay. We have tried the usual things – speeding up the music, changing the lighting, pep talks and so on. The answer my partner and I came up with is to get everyone on the shop floor to concentrate on following the pace of the fastest worker, not the slowest. We also thought that some kind of incentive scheme might be needed."

Right, that sounds good – keep thinking about what you might actually do, and the results you would expect. This is all about outcomes. What would you *dream* of happening? How would you *plan* for that to come about? What else might you need in *reality*?

Let's have a more personal example. Ruth, you were talking about a problem with your daughter.

> "Yes. Sara is nearly twelve, and already she is starting to behave like the typical teenager. She won't do her homework, keep her room tidy, or go to bed in the evening until we have really got angry with her."

What did you and your partner come up with as things that you might do? You were working with Vanessa, weren't you?

> "Quite honestly, we didn't come up with anything new. She is an only child, so she must be learning the behaviour from school or something. She is obviously rebelling, but we are quite good parents. We have tried talking to her about her behaviour, but she won't discuss it."

You put this down as something you could change behaviourally. What did you have in mind?

"Well, it is her behaviour that we want to change. More than that, because we don't seem to be able to talk to her or influence her, working directly to change her behaviour seems the only way. I thought perhaps if we showed her what is expected, she would do it."

OK, let's take that as the *dream* of an outcome. Can you imagine what exactly you might do? Give yourself a number of options – you don't have to tell us what they are. Be as creative as you can. OK, see and feel yourself carrying them out, hear what's being said and see what your daughter's reaction is. Is there something that appears to work? Good, now you can start to *plan* how you would do it in practice, and think about what would happen in *reality*.

What are the skills of coaching? You are usually trying to improve the way your client does something that he or she already does well. You may know something about what they do, and how other people do it differently, but you don't have to have the same skills as the person you are coaching. Nick Faldo's golf coach doesn't play as well as he does.

The coach has a number of resources. You can evoke the client's memories of things he or she has already learned. It may be possible to provide films, books or descriptions of how someone else does it. This could be the result of a *modelling* project. Or you can get the client to invent a new way of performing the skill, and help to create as good a version of that new strategy as possible.

Exercise 8.4: Being a Coach
Let's try some coaching. Think of something you do well, and would like to do better. We don't have any films, tapes or books about that here, so the coaching is going to be entirely from within the resources of you, the Client.

Get together in pairs or threes. One of you will be the Client, the others Coaches. Spend about 10 minutes with each person as Client, and see how much improvement you make.

The Client should tell the Coaches briefly about the skill. Then the Coaches should find out how it could be improved. The kind of areas to question might be:

"Do you know of someone who does this better than you? How do they do it?"

"What else do you know that could help you do this better?"

"What resources do you need in order to do this better? Where would you find them?"

"If you were teaching me to do this, what would you teach me to do?"

"What other ways do you know to do this? What aspects of these could you add to the way that you normally do it?"

As each idea for change comes up, try it on, and find out how it changes the skill you have.

So, are you surprised about how much you learned about something you thought you did well? And how pleased will you be to find how skilfully you have done it the next time?

Directing Effort

Now we can move on to changing behaviour by changing thoughts or beliefs. We could tell or teach people something new. Or maybe we just need to show them that what they are doing doesn't actually meet their outcomes in the situation, so that they will believe that they should do something different. Context is very important. It is useful to stay away from the edge of a 30 metre drop because you believe that falling off it would be dangerous. It is less useful to have the same behaviour, and hold the same belief, at the top of a 30-centimetre step.

Go back to Worksheet 8.1 and choose examples where you want to change behaviour cognitively. OK, who has a business example – Sir John?

> "I want customers to buy whizzers from my company rather than from my competitors. Surveys have shown that some users believe we are too expensive. I want to change this belief and so allow them to buy from us. We should be able to do this by showing that the additional features we offer make our machines good value for money."

So, you have a plan for giving potential customers information. This would presumably involve advertising and other written material. Now you need to move on to finding out what you could say that would get this message across effectively. You will need to *match, pace* and *lead* a variety of people with relatively little in common except that they are buyers of whizzers. One of our themes for today will be how to tell people things in ways that they will accept.

Now, has someone got a change that they want to make in the behaviour of a friend or relation? Vanessa, what is your example?

> "I am on the committee of a social club, which meets once a month. The chairman is very pleasant, and does a lot for the club, but when he runs meetings they seem to take forever. They always start late, the discussion rambles on, and nothing ever seems to get decided. If he is away, his deputy takes the chair, and she does the job very efficiently. What I would like is for him to allow her to run all the meetings. It would be nice to get him to believe that his talents lie elsewhere, which they do. Alternatively, perhaps there is a way of teaching him how to run meetings effectively?"

You will need to decide, perhaps in consultation with the other members of your committee, which would be the best approach. Preview the possibilities, come up with a plan, critique it, and put it into practice. As with all well-formed outcomes, remember to do your ecology checks: how will the changes affect everyone, especially you and the chairman? Keep checking that the plan will meet all your outcomes.

Actually, the situation of having to get someone senior to you to do something different is a very common one. It might be worth getting in some practice. Most of you are likely to have an example on your Worksheet. If not, find one now and add it. The person you want to change is someone you cannot order about, and will have to deal with in the future. It might be a boss, a customer or a neighbour. We'll call that person X.

Exercise 8.5: Believing You Can Do It Better

OK, we are going to do an exercise on directing effort. Get into threes: Director, Model and Facilitator.

The Director will outline the change that you want X to make. Brief the other two on the context and X's processing preferences: the Model should take notes. Then work with them to come up with a plan to change X's thoughts, beliefs or knowledge so that there is a different behaviour.

Now the Model should role-play X. The Director will put the plan into effect, with the Facilitator helping the Director to maintain rapport, use Clean Language and work within X's map of the world.

Then have a short discussion about how effective you think the change process would be in practice. Take about 15 minutes per example, then switch roles – Model to Director, Director to Facilitator and Facilitator to Model. Explore one change each, and then come back together.

Obviously there are some shortcomings in this process. We know that the Model isn't actually X. Thus the change was too easy to make. Many of you noticed that rapport and Clean Language aren't enough to install the change, especially if you are trying to get someone to see things from a different angle, or put a new *frame* round them. Nevertheless, you should have some new ideas about how to approach X in this context next time.

Influencing Activity

Guess what – now we can work on changing behaviour by changing feelings and values. We could influence people or get them to feel a new way about something. Will you feel rewarded for doing it well, or punished for doing it badly? How would you feel about tucking into a thick, juicy rump steak if you were a vegetarian?

If we are going to influence somebody to do something by changing their values or their feelings about it, we need to be sure what their system of values is. We can lead them by following their map of the world. Then, if they are doing something that accords with a value that is fairly low on their hierarchy, we could replace it with an activity that is driven by a higher value. For example, suppose you know someone who is always late for work because of not getting up on time. Relaxing by lying in bed is on their hierarchy of values. A higher value might be earning a living to support their family. You could then point out that getting up and going to work meets a higher value than staying in bed does.

Go back to your Worksheet 8.1 and find examples of influencing action by changing the person's emotions or values. I gather that you found it more difficult to come up with examples of changing someone's behaviour by working on their feelings. It is only likely to work with people you know quite well, or if you make quite crude universal assumptions. It is difficult to get the bus driver to stop for you by appealing to his choice of aftershave. It is more likely to work if you stand in front of the bus and assume that his values are against running you down. Don't forget that influencing can use emotional, moral or spiritual imperatives, making people feel good or bad about what they are doing. If you use moral blackmail, though, how will this affect the relationship?

Can we hear some of your changes for other people? Prudence, what change do you want to make?

"My neighbour lets her dog run in and out all the time. It is a nuisance when it gets into my garden, and has led to several near misses by passing motorists. She doesn't seem to notice. Her view is that the animal needs its space. Could I persuade her to keep the dog at home if I told her that it was putting itself in danger?"

It rather depends on your neighbour's hierarchy of values about her dog. If it is more important to her to give the dog freedom of movement than to keep it safe, then your intervention would not work. You might have to appeal to her other values about the importance of the dog relative to road safety or relations with her neighbours. You will need to find out what her highest values are, and appeal to them.

Amanada, you want to make a change in your own behaviour?

> "Yes. It's a bit like your getting out of bed example. I am very busy, at work and with the band. I never seem to get round to doing the housework. I don't like to see the flat dirty, but there is always something better to do than sweep the floor. How do I change that?"

OK, there are a number of points here. Let's look at your hierarchy of values. There is the value of having a tidy house. How important is it in relationship to your other outcomes – sleeping and eating, earning a living and singing in the band? Perhaps you might look at the value that you would put on the time it takes to do the housework. Would you rather spend this doing something else?

You could see this as a motivation problem. Dream ways of giving yourself rewards for doing the work. Or you could see it as a resource allocation problem. Dream ways that the housework could get done – you might persuade a relative to do it, or pay a cleaner. Give yourself more options. Then you can choose an outcome that takes you in a direction that you *want* to go.

Exercise 8.6: *Using Higher Values*

For now, let's practice our leading skills. Work in pairs as Client and Coach.

The Client should talk for a few minutes about something they would like to do, but never get round to doing. The Coach should elicit the hierarchy of values involved and find out what stops the Client from doing it. This involves following the Client's map of the world.

Discuss what the choices are, and how the change might be made. Then the Coach should lead the Client into making the change.

Then swap roles and repeat the exercise for the new Client.

Did you get some changes? At this stage, it is probably more important to increase the number of options, rather than install any particular one of them.

Leading Conversations

What is leading? I am sure that you have noticed that there comes a point in a conversation when you stop pacing someone else's model and start leading from your own. Sometimes it works – people do what you want them to do. Sometimes it doesn't work, and you notice that you are mismatching and not making your point.

The sequence from matching to pacing to leading can be seamless. Consider the following conversation:

"I can't get on with people."
"Oh, so you can't get on with people?" Matching – including voice tones.
"No."
"Are there particular people you don't get on with?" Pacing – for information.
"No, it is everyone." Notice the polarity response pattern.
"But aren't we getting on now?" Leading – by counter-example.
"Oh." The pattern has been interrupted.

If you are going to direct someone to do something, then your words need to have the right effect. That means that they have to fit within your partner's model of the world. Consider these three leads, and whose models they might fit:

"Get your boots polished."
"You should get your boots polished, sir."
"You will look better if you get your boots polished."

Any of these directions will only be effective in the right context.

We need the right authority, belief or value to appeal to. These are what we find out as we pace. Sir John, you are trying to find ways of selling more whizzers?

"Yes, we want to give customers more information so that they buy whizzers from my company. Some users believe that we are too expensive. I want to change this belief so they will buy from us. We have to show that our features offer them good value for money. So we might tell them that independent research has shown Whizzitts to be the best brand. We might show them how useful the added features are. Or we might tell them how good they will feel about buying a high-quality product. In fact, our new advertisements will have to include all three of these appeals to authority, beliefs and feelings."

Advertisements, like any kind of one-to-many communication, must pace as many people as possible. Some people need to be told; some need to believe; and some need to feel right.

Exercise 8.7 Directive Language

Let's practise our use of directive language. Get into groups of three: Director, Client and Observer.

The Director will decide on some behaviour that he wants from the Client by the end of a short conversation. Please check for ecology – make sure that the change you are trying to make is OK for the Client, for you and for the world! Tell the Observer, but *not* the Client, what the required behaviour is.

The Director should start a conversation on a topic that will give information about the Client's models of authority, beliefs and values. At an appropriate point, the Director should use suitable leverage to get the Client to do the behaviour.

Next the Director should tell the other two what was intended and what was achieved, and they should have a brief discussion on how effective the intervention was.

Then change roles – Director to Observer and Observer to Client, and repeat the exercise in each role. Take about five minutes for each client.

That was easy, wasn't it? You just have to listen, plan and act.

So, to lead behaviour, remember that the existing behaviour and your outcome form part of a process. Consider where you could intervene, and practise generating ways of making the change. Match and pace until you know how and where to make your lead. If the lead doesn't work, choose a new lead, and pace until you are ready to use it. If at first you don't succeed, do something different.

Between now and the next seminar, please review your outcomes on Worksheet 8.1, and add a few new ones. Consider the rules for making outcomes well formed (from Day One), and always check the effect of achieving the outcome on all concerned. Remember that you should consider the outcomes carefully to see if you can resolve them by changing the context or the environment, then dream and plan a number of interventions you could make.

Next week, you will continue to learn how to lead in your communicating, and use your actions and words to change thinking and beliefs.

Day Nine:
Imparting Information

This part of the course is about changing what people think, believe and rationalise. In the same way that we can match and pace language and beliefs, we can lead them. This is what we are going to discuss in this session:

• *Changing Beliefs*
Our beliefs and knowledge are always changing – we hear new things or see situations in a different light. It is unusual for most people to have an outcome of changing a belief directly. We shall find out that it is possible, and look at situations where it is desirable.

• *Effective Teaching*
We shall look at behavioural ways of changing beliefs, including demonstrating. One strong, *limiting belief* is that you can't do something that you need or want to do. Perhaps we can show you how you are doing it.

• *Suggesting Alternatives*
Beliefs may be limiting because you haven't realised how they constrain you. *Verbal reframing* is a technique of asking questions and offering suggestions to show that some beliefs are inconsistent or inappropriate in a given situation. You will look at some examples in which apparently negative situations have a *positive outcome*.

• *Adding Values*
The only way to know whether something will go well is to do it. Or is that true? In order to set an outcome that is well formed we have to know in advance that it will come out right for us. We do this by *Future Pacing* – imagining that it has happened and feeling what that is like. If what you believe contradicts what you value, you can use that feeling to help you to change the belief.

Let's start by discussing some of the outcomes you have analysed on Worksheet 8.1 since the last meeting. Has anybody found some interesting examples or problems? Are there any examples that could be changed by environmental or contextual shifts? John, I think you have resolved a family issue?

"I kept telling my son off for playing football in the garden. He had broken windows in my greenhouse and next door, and the neighbours kept complaining. I asked him why he didn't play with the other boys in the park. He seemed reluctant to go, but seemed happy when I took him there. That was until I turned to go home. Then he raced up and insisted on going home with me. I thought this was odd, because he is old enough to be safe crossing the road, and goes to school on his own. It turns out that he was being bullied by one of the other boys, but only when there were no adults present. I'm working on the bullying problem with his school."

When you try to change behaviours, you may find that the reasons for them are quite complex or obscure. As we move on to beliefs, you will find this increasingly common. Pace through the issue one stage at a time, until you find something you can effectively lead on.

Apricot, you have a point?

"Yes, I have been thinking a bit more about the questions we had about smoking in the office. Companies keep trying to stop smokers by setting rules and physically preventing them from lighting up. Wouldn't it be better if we could find some technique that would brainwash them so that they didn't smoke?"

There are a number of issues there. First, what do you mean by brainwashing? We are here to learn how to lead people to believe and value different things. The changes we are making are usually at the margin of their map of the world – getting them to know or feel something that wasn't part of their experience, or to look at what they do know or feel in a different way. Brainwashing implies replacing what people believe and feel now with a completely new set of ideas, and without their full consent. Even if that fits within your personal values system, would it be generally acceptable?

Second, could you construct a complete new map for someone else that works better than the one they are using now? You might say that you can model and transfer your own beliefs and values, but is that perfect even for you? In any case, it is impossible to model them completely. What would it be like if people had an incomplete set of your beliefs and values and some residual ones of their own? Would they be better to work with?

What we can hope to do is to change their maps, so that the behaviour of smoking becomes inappropriate to them, in terms of their beliefs and values.

Changing Beliefs

We are going to find ways of changing what people think, believe and know. In many ways, this is happening all the time: we are continually exposed to new information (unless we are in an isolation tank). As contexts change, we have to react differently, and update what we believe.

To lead belief changes, we have the same choice of channels as for activity. We can use behavioural, cognitive or emotional tools. If we want to teach people something we can demonstrate it, tell them about it or get them to feel what it is like to know it.

We can find some examples to start us off. PS, you have an outcome about making sales?

"Yes. I want people to believe that our service standards are the best in the industry."

You want people to believe that your service standards are the best in the industry. Why do you want that outcome? How will it help sales and what will it do for the company and the customer if you succeed? Let's have some more details.

"OK. For a start, it's true. Some of the others are appallingly slow in answering the phone and coming out to do repairs. Others have poorly skilled engineers. But high service quality has to be paid for, in the price of our whizzers. If the customers don't allow for that, they hear that our prices are too high. We have to educate them to include the cost of

179

extra downtime and repairs to our competitors' machines. We are talking about being the highest-quality supplier in all our advertising. When we get to speak to the client, we are also expected to be the cheapest, and we are not. If the customer will make an allowance for the cost savings on service, then we are competitive."

That is fine. So how might you get the message across? A behavioural approach would be to *demonstrate* it. Just think of ways in which you can show your clients real examples of the costs to them of your service system and those of other suppliers. Find out what happens on the shop floor when a whizzer breaks down. Get the client to work out the cost of being without one of their whizzers for a day or a week. Demonstrate how much easier it is to work when they are getting high service standards rather than low ones.

The cognitive approach is to change the belief by *argument* or written evidence. Show them the bills. Get them to work through the calculations on their own costing system. List the pros and cons.

For an emotional approach, you need to *influence* the client to accept the value of your service. Get them to feel how it would be if their whizzer broke down in the middle of a vital job and the engineer did not turn up. Take them through a crisis or an emergency. Install the sense of peace of mind that comes with high standards.

Worksheet 9.1:   *Changing Thoughts and Beliefs*

Name/Title	Thought/Belief	Desired Change	Method
1			
2			
3			
4			
5			
6			
7			
8			
9			
10			

> ### Exercise 9.1: Cognitive Outcomes
> Let's continue by writing down some ways of thinking or *beliefs* that you want to change in yourself or in other people. On Worksheet 9.1, write down the name, the belief that is less than optimal, and what you would prefer to think. Take a few minutes on your own to write down as many examples as you can – at least half a dozen. Consider the ecology and context in each case, to make sure they are issues that can be resolved by changing beliefs or knowledge. Then go on to decide where you would intervene – on a behavioural, cognitive or emotional level.
>
> Now, get into pairs. Spend 20 minutes each discussing your examples. Get at least one that can be solved by behaviour, one by language and one by changing feelings or values. Make sure you have checked the context and ecology, and have at least three possible ways of achieving your outcome for each change you want to make.

Effective Teaching

You found out in the last session how to make a change in behaviour behaviourally. It involves *doing* something that makes a difference to someone else. Now we want to change thoughts, beliefs and knowledge. You will have to teach that person a new idea, strategy or way of thinking.

We could demonstrate the idea, strategy or way of thinking, or show them the effects of what is being done wrongly. It might be necessary to bring in a teacher, or you might find that the person already has the belief or knowledge, but has to be reminded of it. As we found last time, though, the first thing is to get some additional ways to achieve the outcome.

Can we have an example? Amanada, you want to add a skill?

"Yes. My boyfriend wants to learn to read and write music. Come to that, I'd like to as well. We both believe that it is difficult, so I suppose that's the limiting belief. Perhaps someone could show us that reading music is easy?"

Well, you have seen plenty of musicians sight-reading. Is it easy for them?

"Yes, but they have probably spent years getting the skill. I haven't got the time to do it that way."

There's another limiting belief. Is there another way to learn to read music without spending a long time on it? Or is there a way that you could learn within the time you have available?

"I can't see any quick way to learn. I suppose we could start going to evening classes, if there are any."

What else would you need to convince you that you could read and write music?

"I suppose that would happen when I was sitting down and doing it."

So, will you discuss that with your boyfriend and turn that into a well-formed outcome?

"OK."

Before you can suggest an intervention, you need to find out what belief is actually the limiting one in the context. Once you have found that, the person you are working with can usually suggest the action that is needed.

Exercise 9.2: Discovering the Limiting Beliefs
Take an example from Worksheet 9.1 that applies to you. Work in pairs as Coach and Client.

The Coach should get the Client to talk about the problem, and point out the limiting beliefs as they arise. Ask the Client for a solution. Notice any further limiting beliefs (listen for "but", "however" and pauses, and look for incongruity signals) and ask for solutions to those. When the solution seems congruent, and there are no more limiting beliefs, ask the Client to turn the solution into a well-formed outcome.

Then change roles, and tackle an issue for the new Client.

For homework, you could do this by writing down the problem and possible solutions, tackling the limiting beliefs as they come up. Make sure you get an agreement signal, as in Exercise 5.3.

Suggesting Alternatives

What might be a good way of changing beliefs verbally? How do *you* change people's minds when you talk to them? Let's write some ideas on the board.

Tell them new facts
Get them to see it differently
Appeal to their higher beliefs
Point out where they are inconsistent
Show them more evidence
Get them to try thinking differently
Point out what will happen if they don't change
Ask them for counter-examples
Get them to see they are not achieving their goals
Teach them a better way to think

That's a good list, and I am sure that you could add more given extra time. Let's look at some of the items. You say that you can make changes by either giving people information they don't have, or by asking them to consider what they already know in a new way. We can ask them to measure their beliefs against the context. You could also bring up for them the behavioural effects of what they believe; the effect is of this belief on their other beliefs; or what effect this belief has on their values. What we are trying to do is to find some leverage to evoke a change. In NLP we call this *reframing*.

Worksheet 9.2: *Positive Outcomes*

1.   He drove his car straight at her and knocked her down.

2.   She told him that he was a louse.

3.   We were hanging, supported by a single, frail cable.

4.   The baby was sick all over his new designer jacket.

5.   When they took it out of the wash, only some of the stains had gone.

6.   Profits in the last quarter have fallen from £10 million to £5 million.

7.   She said that she could never see him again.

8.   The millennium bug has wiped out all the records.

9.   The television is only showing repeats tonight.

10.   I can never learn this technique.

Exercise 9.3: Contextual Reframing

Let's try an exercise. Worksheet 9.2 has a list of things that are normally considered to be negative. Please work together and decide, for each one, a *context* in which the statement would be positive.

OK, let's take the first example: "He drove his car straight at her and knocked her down." Who has some good contexts?

"She pulled the gun and started shooting at him, so..."

"The grizzly bear kept coming at him. To stop her..."

"The timing of the scene was carefully set up, so that it would seem as if..."

That's very good, you all seem to have the idea. Let's go on to the next one: "She told him that he was a louse."

"It was an unusual part in a very strange opera."

"Of course, she actually meant he was from Laos."

"...rather than a flea, so she could marry him after all."

Yes, that is well done. What have you come up with for number 6: "Profits in the last quarter have fallen from £10 million to £5-million."

"That's not bad, considering our Far East losses."

"After writing off the investment in new plant."

"We thought that we might make just £2 million."

Good – we are on a roll here. Let's go for number 8: "The millennium bug has wiped out all the records."

"...at the tax office."

"...of what we owe."

"So we won't have to compete with all the old versions."

And number 10: "I can never learn this technique."

"...I thought, but now I know it well."

"So I'll find a different way to do it."

OK, so what have you done to make the statements positive? The presupposition has changed from "this is a bad thing" to "this is a good thing". You have suggested changing the *place* in many cases – from a road accident to a film set, or from your office to the tax office. It might also be possible to change the *time*, as the last example. Certainly, changing the *people* involved makes a huge difference. Actors, clowns and insects react in different ways to people driving, talking at home or working.

We can ask *where, when* and *with whom* can we use this behaviour, belief or value appropriately? What contexts justify or prohibit it? Where does this rule apply, and where does it not make sense? We need to put a frame of environment and context round what we do, think or feel. If we change the frame, we may need to do, think or feel differently.

Exercise 9.4: Verbal Reframes

Take your Worksheet 9.1 and get together with a partner as Client and Coach.

As Client, take one of your examples and discuss with the Coach why the person with these beliefs is likely to have them. In what context were they right for that person? Choose some alternative beliefs that are right for the new context, and choose the most appropriate one. Then discuss how to lead the person from the old belief and context into the new belief and context.

Change roles and repeat the process for one of the new Client's examples. If there is time, continue to work on further examples alternately. Take 30 minutes in total.

OK, who would like to go first in presenting an example? Vanessa, you had an issue of unreasonable expectations?

"Thank you. This involves people coming for job interviews. Many applicants think that they are worth a higher salary than we are prepared to offer them. There can be quite a number of reasons why people think they are worth more than we can pay them. It might be that they are already earning more than we are offering. Or they may think that their market rate is higher.

"The appropriate context for the belief may just be fantasy. Usually we put the salary range in the advertisement, but even so, some people come to try to negotiate the figure upwards. Sometimes, when I present the full facts – the job, working conditions and other benefits – the applicants change their minds and take the post at the offered rate.

"I'm not sure that there is a lot more that we can do to change the unrealistic beliefs. Obviously, the more clearly we can describe the job and the remuneration – that is, our context – the more unreasonable their belief becomes. So I simply put it to them that they know what the work is, and what they will get for doing it. Of course, sometimes we may have to pay up in order to get the right candidate. Then it has to be a board decision to change the company's belief about what it should pay to get the best employee."

That all sounds pretty comprehensive. It goes to show that changing someone else's belief is likely to involve you changing the way that you behave, think and value. Can we have another example, please? Yes, Paul, you have a family issue?

"Yes. My sister thinks she can tell me how to get on with my girlfriend. She is nearly ten years older than I am, and she played a big part in bringing me up. My mother was in hospital a lot when I was a child, so she did control and advise me in those days. Now she won't leave me alone. I know she is trying to help, but she isn't making the relationship any easier."

So, did you decide between you and Ruth what you wanted her to believe?

"My partner suggested thanking her for what she did in the past. I was a bit reluctant because I didn't want to encourage her to do it in the future. Ruth didn't think that would be the case. I want her to realise that I am responsible for my actions now. I will tell her that I will listen to her advice and then do what I want to do. If she keeps interfering, I will make it obvious that I do not believe in her solutions and will not follow them."

My advice would be to pace her beliefs as far as possible and lead her to believe that you have learned all her lessons. Then she won't have to show or teach you any more. You may also have to help her to direct her belief that she has to teach in some other, more useful direction.

John, can we go back to the problem you were having with your son being scared of bullies? I think you have been working on this again?

"Right. I realised that my son's fear of bullying could be seen as a belief. He seems to have come to very little physical harm. It is mostly threats and taunting, affecting his sense of identity. The bullies have persuaded him that he is weak and powerless, unpopular and 'different' – that's a big negative at his age. I thought that I might use some counter-examples, to show that he is in the same position as everyone else at the school. We talked about it, and decided that his weakest spot is that he is embarrassed by having to wear glasses. Then I realised that the headmaster, who is a bit of a role model for him, also wears glasses. So I thought that I could just point this out."

That's a good idea. Make as strong a connection as you can. Point out that many people that he looks up to also wear glasses. I'm sure several of the others in his class do – maybe even one of the bullies does?

You won't be able to change all the beliefs, and the old ones will still have an impact. Just check – does the new belief help your conversation partner to do what he or she wants to do? Have you invented a new future that makes life easier for that person and those around them?

189

Adding Values

When we use values to change beliefs, we are asking our partner to go into the future, and find out that it feels better having the new belief rather than the old one. We might call this *Future Pacing*. We ask the other person to imagine how it will be after the change.

You each have at least one example of a situation where you want to change someone's belief by contrasting it with his or her values. We might find that the belief directly contradicts a value. For example, they might value individual liberty, and at the same time believe that no one should be allowed to smoke. An appeal to the value is likely to set off some internal processing. You will probably hear a string of "...but ...but ...but". As long as the value is strong, the belief is likely to be qualified or modified. Once you have found the value to appeal to, and allowed the time for the map to be adjusted, then you will need get your partner to go into the future and experience the new belief in context.

Let's have a demonstration. Has someone found an issue where there might be an internal conflict between your beliefs and your deeper values? Prudence, yours is a personal issue?

> "Thank you. It concerns me, but really it is a work issue. I have a belief that I am no good at arithmetic. As Managing Director of Whizzitts Ltd, I have to sign accounts and be responsible for a budget of several million pounds. My personal ethic says that I must do that conscientiously, but I know that I am not checking things properly."

Thank you, Prudence. Can you tell me what being no good at arithmetic means to you?

> "Numbers confuse me. They make me feel ignorant and small. I want to do it right. Now, logically, I can't be doing it right if I let the numbers confuse me. If I am doing it right, the numbers won't confuse me."

OK, stop there a moment. Your underlying value is to do things right, conscientiously. You also believe that numbers confuse you, so this is the limiting belief. Take on the State of Curiosity and Wonder (Exercise 4.5). Now, visualise yourself going through the accounts conscientiously and doing it right. What else do you need in the way of resources?

> "I need someone there to explain the things I don't under-
> stand."

There is someone you can get to do that? And you are willing to ask for explanations? I am getting nods of agreement. Is there anything that might stop you from doing it this way?

> "There are things in the past that stopped me being comfort-
> able with arithmetic. But if I work with the right woman, and
> we go through it step by step, I think that I can cope."

The belief has changed, from "I am confused by numbers" to "I think I can cope". So, Prudence, go into that future situation of working with the accounts again. Allow yourself the support that you need. And do the task conscientiously and right. How was that? I see a big smile and nodding. Thank you, Prudence.

You can often help others to resolve similar difficulties by working out which belief and value are the most important in the situation. Then lead them into the future to make sure that a practical solution is available within their resources.

Exercise 9.5: Valuing Your Beliefs
It is the time to test out some more of your examples and try out visualising the outcome. Please work in threes this time, a Client and two Coaches.

Choose a belief that can be changed by appealing to a higher value. It will be easier for this exercise to use an outcome that you want for yourself.

The Client should brief the Coaches on the context, your belief and values system. Discuss the possible solutions and how you might put them into practice.

The Coaches should elicit the limiting beliefs and the values that are important in the context, as we did in the example with Prudence. Ask the Client to get into the State of Curiosity and Wonder and to visualise being in the situation with the positive values you have just elicited.

Go through the situation, and decide what resources are needed. Find the resources, and check that they fit the ecology – that is, that the Client is happy to use them, and you think they fit the situation. If the Client has doubts, or shows incongruity, make adjustments or try a new approach.

Once you have set up the positive values, and added in the resources, check that the limiting belief has been replaced or over-ridden by a more resourceful one. Finish with a visualisation of a satisfactory outcome to the situation.

Then the Coaches should take turns to be the Client. Come back together when you have each had a chance to clarify one example. If you have some other personal contexts to work on, you can follow the steps of the exercise on your own. You could also do it with members of your family or friends.

Let's just think about how you can now lead people's ideas, thoughts and beliefs. You start by matching and pacing their model of the world. That means you have to act as if you share their ideas and beliefs while finding out more about them. Then, to lead, you want to give them your own information. You have to search for a place where this information might fit, and suggest it in a way that it connects with their system.

So just sit back for a moment and reflect on everything that you have learned today and over the previous eight seminars. As you consider what you now know, take yourself forward to that the point where you have succeeded in improving that vital conversation that you had to get right. See what an impression you are making. Hear the right words coming out, and the appreciative voices. And feel how good it is to be a competent communicator and to have all those extra skills tucked away ready to use.

The next session is our last one. To round off the pattern, we will be learning how to lead feelings and values. There will also be a chance to find out a little more about the background to what we have been doing on this course. See you then.

Day Ten:
Boosting Feelings

In this last session, we are going to find out more about leading *internal states* – values, feelings, emotions, ethics, morality, ideals and the spirit. Here's a summary of what we are going to cover:

● *Leading Values*
If you can change what people value, you have a very powerful tool for *selling* to them. We have already seen that values tend to drive behaviours and beliefs.

● *Training Moods*
If you can *pace* the elements of a person's feelings, the physiology and behaviours, the language and beliefs that go with them, then you can *train* them to be in the right mood to carry out a task.

● *Providing Motives*
How often have you changed the way you *feel* about someone when you learned more about that person? Perhaps you have improved the way you *value* a job when you are told that the payment for it has been doubled. Information is a key to *motivation*. *Reframing* is one way of providing this new information.

● *Giving Inspiration*
Some things are very important to you. Others, which seem similar to an outsider, do not move you at all. You will learn how to use the *hierarchy of values* to make things more important for other people and *propulsion systems* to find things that drive them to accept new states of affairs.

● *Excellent Communicating*
We will recap the course by running through the process by which we all learnt to communicate. When we were babies we could only *lead* by demanding food and attention. As children we developed the skills of *pacing*, to learn from others. Finally, as adults, we have become aware of the importance of *matching* others in order to get closer to them. Now we can use all these techniques *consciously*. You should also be aware of how you can lead others' behaviours, beliefs and values by what you do, say and feel yourself.

● *For the Future*

You have built up some skills for communicating and solving interpersonal problems. Now you can add to them with practice, further courses and reading.

To start today's session, does anyone want to update us on an issue from earlier in the course? Yes, John, you had some more ideas about how to stop your son being afraid of being bullied?

> "Last week, I worked on his dislike of wearing glasses, and gave him some role models who wore glasses. I did some brainstorming and came up with a few more. Then I asked him to walk through the situation wondering how it would be if he were all these people. That had some effect. There still seemed to be something wrong, so I talked to him again, and this time the most important thing was that he thought that he was too puny. We did a short exercise to find out how to overcome that. The best outcomes seemed to be more role models, ways of growing stronger and ways of believing that he was strong enough. We went through the Disney pattern together with all these ideas and came up with a role model who is a martial arts teacher who could help him to get stronger. I booked him an initial lesson."

This sort of example shows us that we should lead from within the other person's map. If the outcome isn't right for your son, he won't achieve it. Changes may be constrained by *internal* capabilities, beliefs and values, whether they are internal to the individual or to the organisation. They can also be stopped by *external* limits – scientific and political laws, or the lack of physical, mental or financial resources.

Leading Values

Potentially, if we can get others to accept our feelings and values, we will also drive their behaviour and beliefs. If we are selling something, and can lead our customers to say "I only feel right buying this brand", then we know that their behaviour and beliefs will follow. They may even sell the product to others: this is the process known as 'word-of-mouth recommendation'.

In terms of relationships, the value 'I love you' will also generate a series of behaviours and beliefs, although the responses will be individual. This can lead to conflict if one party presupposes responses that the other person does not make. You might hear statements such as "He can't love me, he doesn't buy me flowers"or "If she loved me she would always be waiting for me when I get home in the evening".

A lot of conflict is caused this kind of false assumption that a value implies a particular belief or behaviour. The Basic Fractal Language Model connection patterns allow us to analyse what lies behind the misunderstanding.

There may be a number of reasons for wishing to change other people's values. It may be that we want to *influence* them to do something differently. We might want to *motivate* them to learn something. Or we might want to *inspire* them to have a new state, to feel or value things differently.

Exercise 10.1: Emotional Outcomes
So let's find some examples to work with. You know the process by now. Take Worksheet 10.1. For each example, give the name or job title of the person you want to lead, the value you want to change or update, and what you would prefer them to feel. Take a few minutes on your own to write down as many examples as you can – at least half a dozen. Consider the ecology and context in each case, to make sure they are issues that can be resolved by getting the person to feel or value the issue in a better way. Then go on to decide where you would intervene – on a behavioural, cognitive or emotional level.

Now, get into pairs. Spend 20 minutes each discussing your examples. Get at least one that can be solved by influencing behaviour, one by using motivating language and one by inspiring changes in feelings or values. Make sure you have checked the context and ecology, and have at least three possible ways of achieving your outcome for each change you want to make.

Worksheet 10.1: Changing States and Values

Name/Title	State/Value	Desired Change	Method
1			
2			
3			
4			
5			
6			
7			
8			
9			
10			

Training Moods

We'll go straight on to making changes in feelings or values by how we behave. Can we have an example, please? You have a business example for us, Apricot?

> "Yes. When we get new members of staff, it takes them quite a long time to settle down and become productive. We need to find a way of making them feel at home. We haven't brainstormed this yet, but my idea is to behave better towards them."

OK, let's start with some pacing. Is there anyone here who has recently changed jobs and come to a new office? Paul, are you the new boy? Come and sit at the front.

We will start by finding out from Paul what is different for him about being a new member of staff. Paul, could you go back to a time when you were working well in a job you had had for some time. Be aware of what that is like, the pictures, sounds and sensations that come to mind, the important beliefs, the feelings and the emotional states.

Now, can you remember the first day in your current job, coming into a new company, with a new office and new people? Go back to that day. Be aware of what that is like, the pictures, sounds and sensations that come to mind, the important beliefs, the feelings and the emotional states.

Just to check the contrasts, go back to first state, when you were working well. What are the important differences between the two experiences in terms of representations, beliefs and states?

> "In the new job, I was nervous, and more aware of what was going on around me. The pictures and sounds were all sharper and closer. Instead of a warm feeling in my stomach, there was a lump in my chest. I had to react faster, and I did not know what to expect. I felt as if I was being tested."

OK, now we'll try Apricot's suggestion. Go back to your first day in this job. Now you can change the way the other people around you were behaving. If it helps, you can change anything from the time you applied for the job, the interviews or whatever. Try some alternatives, then come back and tell us what would have made your state closer to the one in the first experience of working well.

> "I tried quite a lot of changes. The only one that seemed to make much difference was when the other people in the office were matching me. Then they started to fade into the background and I felt more comfortable."

As a group, I guess that most of you were following through the instructions, and feeling for yourselves what being in a new job is like. Does anyone have any different answers to the question? Is there any other way that the existing staff in the office should behave? Apricot, how does putting your suggestion into action work for you?

> "I think I'll have to agree with Paul. I looked through a number of possible changes such as being friendly or helpful. None of them really gave me the right state. We shall have to go back and teach all our people matching skills."

So, let's use this process of contrasting states to check out some of the examples you have come up with.

Exercise 10.2: Ideal States

Work in pairs, Model and Coach. The Coach should choose one of her examples of changing a subject's state by doing something different to or around him.

Pace the Model into the *ideal* state – get him to recall an experience when he was in the right context and state. Ask him to be aware of what that was like, what he saw, heard and sensed, the important beliefs, the feelings and the emotional states.

Then pace the Model into the state that needs changing. Ask him for a *reference* experience – one that is as close to the state you are trying to change as he has available. Again, ask him to find out what that was like, what he saw, heard and sensed, the important beliefs, the feelings and the emotional states.

Return the Model to the *ideal* state and ask him for the differences in representations, beliefs and feelings.

Now ask the Model to go back to the *reference* experience. Pace him with the behavioural changes that you want to make and find out what difference that makes to the state.

Change roles, keeping the same example. The new Coach should take the new Model through her experiences. Find out whether her reaction to the behavioural changes is the same as yours.

Then repeat the exercise with an example from the list of the new Coach.

Did anyone find a good way of changing a state with a behaviour? Amanada – you and Sir John tried out a classical method of changing mood, didn't you?

> "Yes. My example was that when I get stuck writing a letter, I could put on a record and dance to change my state and become more creative. We paced stuck and creative states, then I asked Sir John to imagine being in the stuck state, putting on a record and dancing to it. We had to find a safe context: I could see Sir John wasn't too happy about doing this in the office! He tried out several different types of music, and saw himself dancing to them. This had quite an impact, and could generate new ideas. I know this technique works, because I use it myself. I found out that pretending you are listening to music and dancing also works well, so you could use it in the office."

I know others of you were experimenting with all kinds of exercise, massage and physiological changes. States have a physical and physiological component. If you change that, you will change the state. You can keep experimenting to find out what works for you, and others around you.

Providing Motives

Let's move on to changing someone's feelings or values by giving them some information or a belief. This is a classic selling technique: "You will feel good about buying my product when you know more about it." The question is what I should tell you about it.

Can you give us some other examples where you want to make a change in state by changing knowledge or beliefs? Yes, PS, you have a sales example?

> "No, it's more a personal one. I find I can't concentrate well in long meetings. I've tried to learn from others how to do it, and I've read the books, but nothing seems to work. If I really believed that I could concentrate, then I would be OK."

Let me ask you a few questions. How long do you want to concentrate for?

> "About an hour and a half."

And how long do you find you *can* concentrate for?

> "Maybe 45 minutes."

So what would you need to be able to concentrate for two consecutive periods of 45 minutes?

> "Oh, ah, a break of state. I'd need to have a change. Get up and walk around. Have a cold beer, or a cup of tea. Go out and talk to my secretary. I could do lots of things."

Did you all notice what happened in the pause before that burst of ideas? PS showed signs of doing a lot of internal processing, when I reminded him that a long period of time is the same as two shorter periods of time added together. And he knows how to link these two periods of time. Believing that he could concentrate for two short periods of time has replaced the limiting belief that he could not concentrate for a long period of time.

This is an example of *reframing*. On Day Nine we discussed contextual reframing. Now we can extend this to time, space and matter. You can transfer a resourceful belief about one time, place or thing to replace a limiting belief. What PS believes about a period of 45 minutes is also true for him about two consecutive periods of 45 minutes, as long as they are properly separated.

We are talking about motivating – giving people a reason to change their feelings or values. It might be something quite minor to change a temporary mood: telling a joke, for example. It would have to be a pretty powerful reason to change a major life value like pacifism. In principle, the reason could be any sort of language pattern or piece of information (true, false or fantasy). The aim is to get the person you are talking to, or who is reading what you have written, to reconsider their feelings or values in the light of what you have told them.

Let's hear another of your examples where you want to change your own state. Prudence, you told us last time that you felt confused by numbers. You got the problem to the state of "I think I can cope". Would you like to take this a stage further now? She is nodding. OK, Prudence, please tell us about a situation where you are comfortable with numbers.

> "It's OK for household things. Knitting patterns, lottery tickets and supermarket bills don't worry me – unless the numbers are too big. I don't know what would happen if I was to win the lottery."

So, when is a number too big? What is a comfortable number?

> "Shopping bill numbers are fine. I can hang on to amounts of £100 or so. Once it gets up into the thousands I begin to lose touch. My monthly salary cheque – well, sometimes I wish that I was paid weekly – it's difficult for me to think of that much as real. I leave my husband to deal with pensions, investments, and cars, that sort of thing. When it comes to company accounts, with figures in the millions, it doesn't mean anything to me."

OK. When you work with comfortable amounts, you have something you can touch – the goods the money buys or the number of stitches in a row of knitting. You can't grasp everything that your monthly salary would buy, or the figures in a set of accounts.

Let's find out what things various sums of money could buy around the company – just call out your suggestions:

£1,000	**– a desktop computer, a desk and chair**
£5,000	**– a photocopier, the furniture in an office**
£10,000	**– a car, the design office computer**
£50,000	**– an assembly line, a delivery truck**
£100,000	**– the new assembly building extension, all the machinery in it**
£500,000	**– the office block, a container-load of whizzers**

Now, Prudence, I don't know what numbers there are in your accounts, but let's say that the company has monthly sales of £4 million and costs of £3.5 million including a wage bill of £200,000. Compared with the budget, sales are up £20,000 and profits are £7,000 better. Could you hang on to those numbers better if you thought of sales being eight container-loads of whizzers, and the wage bill enough to pay for the new assembly building and the machinery in it? The budget variances mean that the extra sales would buy two cars, and the extra profit is enough to pay for the photocopier, computer, desk and chair in your secretary's room? I'm getting some more nods.

Thank you for being a guinea pig, Prudence. To do this reframing we need to find what is different between the good state and the bad state. For Prudence, comfortable numbers were ones that she could *touch*, either directly or through a simple process of remembering the items in her shopping bag. She could not deal kinaesthetically with larger numbers. What we did was to give her a set of objects to represent various large sums of money, and put her in touch with them.

Look at your Worksheet 10.1 and choose an example where you want to change a feeling or value by altering a belief. Use one that refers to you or to someone whose values and beliefs you have thoroughly paced and whose role you can play. Take a situation where you want to move from an unresourceful state to a better one.

Exercise 10.3: Reframing Beliefs

Work in pairs, Client and Coach. The Coach asks the Client to describe the cause of the *poor* state in the first person – as if it is *your* situation, state and beliefs.

The Coach should then ask for similar experiences where you are in a *good* state. Notice the differences in language and beliefs between the two situations. If the differences are not clear, ask for another example of a similar good state.

Once you have the contrast, reframe the poor state in terms of the language and resourceful beliefs of the good one. Ask or calibrate whether the state has changed. You may need to try several different approaches before you find the one that allows the Client to think about the situation in a different way.

Then switch roles and work on an example for the new Client.

Has anyone found a useful reframe that they would like to pass on? Stephen, what have you discovered?

"My Client wanted to know how she could remember to pay the household bills on time. It turned out that the real problem was that she did not see any benefits as a result of paying for standard services, and so just put off sending the cheques. She did not mind settling restaurant bills or paying for clothes, because she had seen and enjoyed the product. We discussed two possible approaches. One was to put the bills out of sight as well, by arranging direct debit payments. The other was to appreciate the benefits. I asked her to visualise coming into a house in darkness (with no electricity), cold (no gas) and with bailiffs chasing her up the road, in contrast to having everything working properly. Judging by the body language, the direct debit route may be more likely to succeed."

That's an interesting set of reactions. Some people are more influenced by moving *towards* something good, others by moving *away from* something bad. You will learn how to use this effect later on today.

Giving Inspiration

When we use emotional tools for influencing values, we have a number of possible leads. You could ask people how they feel about their values in a particular context. It might be possible to teach them a new value by demonstrating the way it affects you, or by a full modelling process. Or you could invoke a higher-level value to get someone to change the way he or she feels about a situation.

Remember that people carry a lot of values and feelings around with them. They may call them faith or spirituality, moral laws or precepts, conscience or ethics. From the outside you might classify them as a personality profile, a hierarchy of values or a range of moods. These are potentially in conflict in any context, and you may well be able to point to one that gets the person you are communicating with feeling the way you intend.

> *Exercise 10.4: Inspiring Values*
> Get together in pairs, Model and Coach.
>
> Imagine you are at home on Sunday morning. The Model should talk about values and feelings in that situation. The Coach should take notes. When you have a reasonable list (say four or five), establish the hierarchy by asking "Is this more important than that?"
>
> Now the Coach should choose a value that is not on the list. Make it something that is plausible in the circumstances. Attempt to install it at the top of the hierarchy of values. Work it up the list by equating it to the least important existing value and then using emotional arguments to make it more important.

Next, the Coach should choose a context where the new value would be very low in the hierarchy, or have a negative affect. Pace the Model into the new context and check that the value has moved down.

Then change roles and repeat the exercise for the new Model.

Would you like a demonstration of this exercise before you try it out? Could we have a volunteer, please? Sir John, come and sit at the front here, please. Now, it is Sunday morning and you are at home. What are you doing? And in this situation, what is important to you?

> "I'm reading the Sunday paper in front of the fire. My wife is in the kitchen preparing lunch – my son and his family are coming round. My family is obviously important, having a comfortable house and a good lunch. There's a feeling of having time to myself."

Thank you, Sir John. You have mentioned four values: your family, a comfortable house, a good lunch, and time to yourself. So, if you could have either your family or a comfortable house, but not both, which would you choose?

> "My family, definitely."

(We continue to question Sir John about each of his six pairs of values in a manner similar to that described in Exercise 4.9, page 90)

So we have completed your hierarchy of values, which is:
1.   Your family
2.   Time to yourself
3.   A comfortable house
4.   A good lunch

Let's choose another value that isn't particularly important to you in this situation, say 'peace of mind'. If you don't mind, I'll comment to the rest of the group on *the reactions that Sir John makes to what I am saying*. So, Sir John, could you enjoy a good lunch if you were worried about something important? *Sir John looks down, and his smile droops. He reluctantly disagrees.* So, in fact, peace of mind is at least as important as having a good lunch? *Sir John looks up, his smile returns and he nods.* And indeed, Sir John, can you be comfortable in any house when there is something weighing on your mind? *Again, he looks down and admits that he would not be comfortable in that situation.* So, peace of mind is at least as important as having a comfortable house. *There is physiological and verbal agreement.* Now, Sir John, let's assume it is Sunday morning, and you have plenty of time to yourself, but you are worrying that one of your children might be in trouble. You can only brood. *He nods.* You have to agree that peace of mind is at least as important as having time to yourself. *Sir John agrees.* But perhaps the thing that is worrying you isn't about a member of your family. Perhaps it is something that is even more important to you – it might be your health, or the state of the economy, or the fate of your soul. *With each suggestion, I am calibrating the strength of the physiological response. The strongest reaction was to the issue of health.* So, you have your family around you, but you are worried that you are going to die. Could it be that getting peace of mind about your health might be even more important than your family? *Sir John reluctantly agrees. That completes the first part of the exercise. Now I am going to change the context and make the value less important.*

I know you enjoy a game of squash, Sir John. Imagine you are on the court with a deadly rival, and the scores are tied. How important to you is peace of mind? *There is a pause while Sir John searches for an answer.*

> "There are too many other things going on to worry about peace of mind."

Thank you, Sir John. *That completes the second part of the exercise, leaving the Model in the new situation and having made the inserted value unimportant again.*

Now please try that in your pairs.

You should be able to work out for yourselves how these techniques could be used to lead some of the values in your examples on Worksheet 10.1. Try them for real when you get a chance.

Some people are naturally inclined to find a positive reason for doing things. They know what they want and they go for it. Others generally react against things, and move away from situations that they do not like. In practice, our reasons are rarely about simply going towards or simply moving away from things. There is usually a mixture of attractive and repulsive drivers.

Exercise 10.5: Propulsion Systems

Let's find a few of those drivers for ourselves. Start by working out, on your own, an *outcome* that you have, to do with money. Make the outcome well formed, and write it at the top of a sheet of paper.

Now, we'll find your drivers and turn those into a propulsion statement. Get together in pairs, Model and Coach. The Coach will need to take notes on the Model's outcome sheet.

The Model should talk for a few minutes about values to do with *money*. The Coach should note the ones that describe towards and away-from drivers. Aim to get at least four in each list. You may have to prompt the Model if all the values go in the same direction. Then get the hierarchy of values for towards and away-from drivers separately.

Next, the Model should talk about his or her values concerning the *family* and family life. The Coach should note the ones that describe towards and away-from drivers. Aim to get at least four in each list. You may have to prompt the Model if all the values go in the same direction. Then get the hierarchy of values for towards and away-from drivers separately.

Now the Coach should list the top towards and away-from drivers for money, and the top towards and away-from drivers for the family. Spend a few minutes writing a statement about the outcome so that all four of the top drivers (about money and the family) can be brought to bear on it. Then feed the propulsion statement back to the Model and calibrate the reaction.

Then change roles, and go through the exercise for the new Model. Take about 30 minutes for each outcome.

Let's hear some examples. Yes, Paul, this was Ruth's issue? OK, tell us the outcome, the drivers and the propulsion statement.

> "The outcome was: "To spend £10 a month less on telephone bills by calling at weekends rather than in the week." Her top four drivers are: Money, towards – "having a comfortable standard of living"; Money, away-from – "not getting into debt"; Family, towards – "doing the best for my daughter"; and Family, away-from – "avoiding bad feelings". This was the propulsion statement I gave her. "You really want to do the best for your daughter and have a comfortable standard of living without getting into debt. There are more important things to spend money on than telephone bills, and you could save £10 a month by calling at weekends rather than in the week. You will, of course, have to be careful that this outcome doesn't cause any bad feelings in the family." She seemed to take that well – smiling and nodding."

Yes, that's good. It should set in a value about when to use the phone that wasn't there before.

Sometimes you may be able to elicit the values directly, and enquire about the hierarchy. More often, you will need to pick up the values from a more general conversation – steering it on to the areas you need information about as necessary, and calibrating which ones are the most important. Choose the values systems to pace so that they cover the area that you want make changes in. Pace the value that you wish to install to be as close to existing values as possible. Then use a propulsion statement and calibrate the result.

Again, this is something you will want to work up to in a real situation. You should practise listening for driver values and calibrating which of them are important to the person you are communicating with. You can also develop a repertoire of ways of setting outcomes for others and framing them with drivers.

Excellent Communicating

Some years ago, you learned to communicate. As a baby, you only needed to *lead*, and only in very general terms. There would be anxious adults about to interpret the meaning of your cries, and do whatever you wanted. Once you had learned some language, it was easier to ask for what you wanted. Paradoxically, though, you were less likely to get it immediately, especially if you didn't remember to use the magic words 'please' and 'thank you'. You learned to *pace* others, to know what they expected you to say and do before your wishes would be met. *Matching* and modelling you probably learned unconsciously. You copied other people who were successful. It became clear that it was easier to talk to someone if you shared language, beliefs and values: you probably didn't notice that this also made you behave and talk like them.

Over ten modules, we have recapitulated this process, but in reverse. We started from a theoretical level to find out why we communicate what we do, how we structure the communication and what we actually say or write. Then we built up a new understanding of our communicating, working with tools to improve our matching, pacing and leading in holistic ways which include physiology and behaviour, thoughts and beliefs, feelings and values.

As you have gone through this course, you have become conscious of how this process of matching improves the way you communicate with other people. You have found out how much you learn about them by asking simple, clean questions. You have also found how easy it is to lead them to your outcomes if you respect their behaviour, beliefs and values.

In the last three sessions, we have analysed many practical problems and suggested conversational ways to lead the people we are with into new ways of doing, thinking or feeling. Those of you who haven't yet tried the techniques for real now have a wide range of tools and language, and a good deal of experience, to allow you to do just that. Remember that you can lead to change what someone else does, thinks or feels. You can achieve the outcome by modifying the context, by your own behaviours, by saying something or evoking a new state or value in the person you want to influence.

213

Remember that people are not all the same. Their models of the world differ from yours. They have different preferences for lead predicates, chunk size, sorting and almost anything else you can think of. Their beliefs and values are personal. So when your outcome is to lead them, you must have a good idea where you are leading them in terms of their map.

There is an alternative. Remember that we are trying to give ourselves choices, not dilemmas. If you work on your language so that it is artfully vague, you can match most people. You know what you know and what you can use. Give yourself opportunities and options. And relax, it will make it easier. You can use all these techniques now, or when you have practised them further. Just remember that people are generally happier when they can agree with you. You can reduce the gap between you by quoting their words back to them. Get into rapport and match well before you even try to pace for further information. Have an outcome for leading before you do it. Lead into agreement, and if you don't get it, go back and match and pace some more.

You have been communicating for a long time, and doing it well. If you continue to practise the techniques in this course, you can do it excellently. And as you look back from the end of that important and successful meeting, just think of all the techniques you used, consciously or unconsciously, to achieve your outcome. Consider briefly how much better it is to communicate from a position of knowledge. Be aware of the ways that you changed on the course, and how much easier it all is now.

For the Future

There is much more we could have learnt about communicating. We could have picked up more NLP techniques, and done a lot more practice. You have spent most of the time working on face-to-face communicating with one other person: we have only touched on group work and written material. No exercises have been done on the possibilities for telephone conversations, radio or television or on presentations in general. Some of these you may be able to work out from what we have done here, but much remains for future study.

You will learn more about communication excellence as you practise the techniques. You can do this with your family, friends or colleagues, but you might also want to do it more formally on an NLP course or at an NLP practice group.

If you would like to contact the author with questions, or would like to talk about courses, coaching or consultation, you can get in touch through the publishers, or send an e-mail message to:

ian.mclaren@cableinet.co.uk

Annotated Bibliography

Alder, Harry (1996). *NLP for Managers*, London, Piatkus Books.
An introduction to Neuro-Lingusitic Programming written from a British business background, particularly the sections on communications and strategy.

Andreas, Steve & Faulkner, Charles (1994/1996). *NLP: The New Technology Of Achievement*, London, Nicholas Brealey Publishing.
This is a recent American book, concentrating on self-help aspects of NLP. It is useful on states such as motivation, confidence and self-appreciation; and on mission and goal setting.

Ardui, Jan & Wryca, Peter (1994). "Unravelling Perceptual Positions", *NLP World*, Vol 1, No 2. Orzens, Switzerland, G. Peter Winnington.
Clarifies how we think of ourselves in relation to others.

Audi, Robert (1998). *Epistemology: A Contemporary Introduction To The Theory Of Knowledge*, London, Routledge.
A philosopher's approach to what we know and how we know it.

Bandler, Richard & Grinder, John (1975). *The Structure Of Magic: A Book About Language And Therapy*, Palo Alto, California, Science and Behavior Books.
The original book about NLP, dealing in particular with what we say and how it can be interpreted.

Bateson, Gregory (1972). *Steps To An Ecology Of Mind*, New York, Ballantine Books.
The sourcebook for the structure of learning and processing information.

Bodenhamer, Bob & Hall, L. Michael (1997). *Time Lining: Patterns For Adventuring In "Time"*, Carmarthen, Wales, Crown House Publishing.
This is the most recent book on how we represent and use the concept of time in NLP.

Cameron-Bandler, Leslie (1985). *Solutions: Enhancing Love, Sex, And Relationships*, Moab, Utah, Real People Press.
Useful background to gaining rapport and gathering information from others.

Cameron-Bandler, Leslie & Lebeau, Michael (1986). *The Emotional Hostage: Rescuing Your Emotional Life*, Moab, Utah, Real People Press.
How to recognise and work with emotions.

Charvet, Shelle Rose (1995). *Words that Change Minds: Mastering The Language Of Influence*, Dubuque, Iowa, Kendall/Hunt Publishing Company.
The questions to ask about values and directions of thought.

Cialdini, Robert B. (1985/1988). *Influence: Science And Practice*, London, HarperCollins Publishers.
A classic work on the psychology of how we are influenced by metaphors, pictures, stories and authority figures.

Dilts, Robert (1994). *Strategies Of Genius: Volume I – The Thinking Processes of Aristotle, Mozart, Walt Disney and Sherlock Holmes*, Capitola, California, Meta Publications.
Includes the Disney Creativity Process.

Dilts, Robert; Grinder, John; Bandler, Richard & DeLozier, Judith (1980). *Neuro-Linguistic Programming: Volume I – The Study Of The Structure of Subjective Experience*, Capitola, California, Meta Publications.
The basis for all NLP interventions – design, structuring, implementation, utilisation and installation.

Jacobson, Sid (1996). *Solution States: A Course In Solving Problems In Business With The Power Of NLP*, Carmarthen, Wales, Crown House Publishing.
How to choose and get into a good state to achieve your outcomes.

Johnstone, Keith (1979/1997) *Impro: Improvisation And The Theatre*, London, Methuen.
Exercises for improving your state and skills when making presentations.

Laborde, Genie Z. (1984/1995). *Influencing With Integrity: Management Skills For Communication And Negotiation*, Carmarthen, Wales, Crown House Publishing.
The original book applying NLP skills to a business context.

McMaster, Michael & Grinder, John (1993). *Precision: A New Approach To Communication*, Scotts Valle, California, Grinder, DeLozier & Associates.
A business approach to outcomes and language.

McWhirter, John (1999). "Re-Modelling NLP, Part II – Remodelling Language", *Rapport*, 44. Stourbridge, West Midlands, Association for Neuro-Linguistic Programming.
The first published article on the Fractal Language Model and its history.

O'Connor, Joseph & McDermott, Ian (1997). *The Art Of Systems Thinking: Essential Skills For Creativity And Problem Solving*, London, Thorsons.
This book helps you to structure your solutions, and to be aware of the systems that they affect.

O'Connor, Joseph & McDermott, Ian (1996). *Principles of NLP*, London, Thorsons.
A short introduction to the terminology and elements of NLP.

O'Connor, Joseph & Seymour, John (1990/1993). *Introducing Neuro-Linguistic Programming: Psychological Skills For Understanding And Influencing People*, London, The Aquarian Press
A good starting point for finding out the basic principles of NLP from a British viewpoint.

Watzlawick, Paul; Weakland, John; & Fisch, Richard (1974). *Change: Principles Of Problem Formation And Problem Resolution*, New York, W. W. Norton & Company.
This book uses examples drawn from psychotherapy to point out that the obvious way of making changes may not be the most effective.

Woodsmall, Wyatt (1999). "'Logical Levels' and Systemic NLP", *NLP World*, Vol 6, No 1. Orzens, Switzerland, G. Peter Winnington.
Developing the relationship between beliefs and values.